Martin Luther

Jim

. G. Wells

John Stuart Mill

Thomas Aquinas

Tolstoy

Napoleon

Virgil

Dante

# EVERYMAN'S DECISION

Lew Wallace

Pontius Pilate

Alfred Lord Tennyson

Calvin

F. F. Bruce

Simon Greenleaf

Charles Dickens

Homer

Ramond Demadian

Lord Byron

Whittier

Elizabeth Kublar Ross

Shakespeare

Josh McDowell

Betty Eady

Norman Mailer

Rousseau

Wiesal

Billy Graham

John Bunyon

Thomas Carlyle

Bronowski

Bertrand Russell

Norman Vincent Peale

Emerson Fosdick

Gladstone

Scott O'Grady

Victor Frankel

Milton

# EVERYMAN'S DECISION

Charles Lamb

Abraham Lincoln

Quadritis

By

**Dr. Lucille Galloway Jordan**

N. T. Wright

Paul, the Apostle

Tacitus

Socrates

Nelson Gueck

Goethe

Lewis Goldberg

Paul De Kruif

James Kennedy

Julian, the Apostate

Chuck Colson

Dave Dravecky

1stBooks – rev. 03/29/00

# About the Book

EVERYMAN'S DECISION deals with the verification of Jesus Christ's place in world history; His purposes, His life, death and resurrection; and His continuing influence on every person's life and death, whether or not He is personally accepted by that individual. Four major faith questions have been widely researched and reported by the author, because it was observed that these are the questions that seekers find most troublesome.

In seeking answers to these questions, the author for years gathered quotes of persons from all areas of life and periods of time from 300 B.C. to the present about Jesus. Reported are over 100 statements from literary and military figures, historical and legal authorities, politicians, theologians, athletes, atheists, agnostics, believers, and non-believers. Through creditable life experiences, and frequently a personal relationship with Jesus, these persons share their gift of insight regarding preponderant faith questions regarding Jesus.

This book is titled <u>EVERYMAN'S DECISION</u> because the classic old English morality play, <u>EVERYMAN</u>, so clearly exemplifies the commonality of all humans throughout recorded history. The concept of EVERYMAN is representative of the human struggle in decision making, and in survival, and it remains the most powerful and most realistic version of the human spirit's struggle with death.

Throughout the book evidence is presented to aid the reader to formulate a decision about Jesus. As he seeks truth, he asks, can all these knowledgeable, and often inspired, believers be wrong? Could all those descriptions of the Messiah made by inspired prophets in the Old Testament be disregarded? Could all of these prophesies be fulfilled in one life at the probability of one in 100,000,000.000,000,000,000 be strangely incorrect? It is beyond all reason!

And so <u>EVERYMAN</u> now realizes that he nor no man can escape answering the 2000 year-old question of Pontius Pilate:
"What shall I do with Jesus?"

# Commendations

Dr. Lucille Jordan has compiled a veritable gold mine of information and inspiration. She writes of her own experience and love of Jesus Christ, and she writes so that others might know that same love. Her presentation of good research and of so many witnesses shows that faith in Christ is not a blind faith, but a faith based on sound evidence.

I commend this volume to all serious seekers, as well as to all honest doubters. It will clarify as well as challenge. I commend this treatise to young and old, to believers and unbelievers, to religious and non-religious. I commend <u>Every Man's Decision</u> with the sincere hope that many will read it and benefit from it.

Dr. Daniel Vestal
President, Cooperative Baptist Fellowship
P. O. Box 450329
Atlanta, Georgia 31145-0329

You will reflect, think, and ponder as you read <u>Everyman's Decision</u>. Dr. Lucille Jordan is uniquely qualified to present with clarity, solid intellectual reasons for faith in God. To make a proper decision, one must become acquainted with what is factual. As you read this book, you will discover many compelling facts. If you are searching for an authentic faith, you will find it in <u>Everyman's Decision</u>.

Reverend Theodore O. Murphy
Regional Representative
Billy Graham Evangelical Association
2665 Favor Road, #2C-1
Marietta, Georgia 30060

Dedicated to the memory

of

My Parents:

The late Thomas P. and Mamie Fisher Galloway who are responsible for my Christian upbringing and for the preservation of our family's rich religious heritage

# ACKNOWLEDGMENTS

First and foremost, appreciation must be acknowledged for the inspiration of my ancestry, maintained through numerous generations by both the paternal and maternal family lines for the over 250 years that they have been in America.

Without the encouragement of numerous associates--my sister, Montaree Galloway Glazener, and my husband, Frederick L. S. Jordan-- I would have left my collection of quotes about Jesus in the files with little thought of publication.

Without the computer skills and constant support of my professional associate, Mary Helen Blair, this manuscript would never have been completed.

My deep appreciation for all of these contributions can be acknowledged, but never fully expressed.

# PREFACE

The title of this manuscript, <u>Everyman's Decision</u>, was chosen because the classic old English morality play, <u>Everyman</u>, so clearly exemplifies the commonality of all men throughout recorded history.

The concept of <u>Everyman</u> as representative of the human struggle in decision making and in survival actually dates back to the 15th century and was first chronicled in a Dutch play, of the same title, by an unknown author.

Modern audiences respond to the austere, dramatic power of <u>Everyman</u> for it remains the most powerful and the most realistic, modern version of the human spirit's struggle with death.

Today the personified abstractions, which are the characters, seem no less real. They speak to us in the realization that the struggle for the soul of man is even keener, is less an abstraction than ever, in our modern technological world. <u>Everyman's</u> confusion and shattered values are our own.

I am not a theologian, but an educator and a lay Christian who has for many years sought answers to some preponderant questions related to my faith. Hence, the reader will note an unusual amount of reference quotation, for I found acceptable, logical explanations often through the creditable experience of not only theologians but also of other seekers. I am grateful for their gift of insight and have noted each reference so that other researchers may avail themselves of more comprehensive study of the resources that I found so meaningful.

Lucille Galloway Jordan<br>
Atlanta, Georgia<br>
December 1997

# CONTENTS

# EVERYMAN'S DECISION

## <u>INTRODUCTION</u>

Since God made His first covenants with man via Noah and Abraham, <u>Everyman</u> must make the decision of whether he accepts life and the hereafter on his own terms or God's. Following Jesus's declaration that He, as God's son, was sent to redeem mankind from his continuous disregard for God's law and to make a new covenant with man, <u>Everyman</u>, as did Pilate, must decide what to do with Jesus and the new covenant that He offered.

As crime, violence, and immorality stalk our streets, and we see the moral center of the world society breaking apart, we have all sensed that as nations and cultures, and all too often as individuals, we are losing our way. We question what has brought about such a dilemma, for no doubt many factors are involved.

A major reason, if not <u>the</u> major reason, is the abandonment of the enduring values which come from the biblical scriptures. We have not abandoned God's word because of lack of evidence. That evidence is overwhelming. We have rejected Him because we do not want to keep His commandments and walk in His ways. We have rejected Him for moral, sinful reasons rather than intellectual ones. When men abandon God, sooner or later they become depraved. It happened in the Garden of Eden, in Sodom, in Ninevah; it happened in the days of Noah preceding the flood; it happened in Rome, and it is happening today.

When we willfully alienate ourselves from God and He still cares for us, we assume a tremendous load of debt to Him and at the same time we have nothing with which to pay. Also, when we fall prey to forces in life that we cannot fight, as those prevalent in our society today, we desperately look for someone to ransom us and set us free.

Throughout all recorded history, human nature has changed only through a spiritual experience--often following much suffering--and a return to God's ways comes as a last resort measure.

As a result of this dilemma, we are seeing a deluge of feature stories, books, movies, and television programs and hearing lectures

1

and seeing general press coverage probing such topics as the search for values, the role of angels, how significant is prayer, and who is Jesus. According to Paul Boyer (a historian at the University of Wisconsin who wrote the book, When Time Shall Be No More, published by Harvard University Press), there is much popular interest in millennial themes and references to soothsayers' predictions, such as Nostradamus's prediction 450 years ago, "In the year 1999 and seven months, the Great King of Terror will come from the sky."[1] Also, Jean Dixon predicted that by 1999 a descendant of Queen Nefertiti will come to power and unite the world.

There is a definite upsurge of interest in God and the things of the spirit and a fast-growing interest in evangelism according to George Carey, the Archbishop of Canterbury. Ron Graham, the Canadian author of God's Dominion: A Skeptic's Quest, expresses the belief that these concerns and interests are a continuing evidence that life's great questions of being, meaning, behaving, and dying can never go away.

"A lot has changed in the last century," says Charles Nicholls, an anthropologist at Emory University who studies religion and healing. "We've stripped away what our ancestors saw as essential--the importance of religion and family. People feel they want something they have lost, and they don't remember what it is they've lost. But it has left a gaping hole. That in essence is the seeker's quest: to fill the hole with a new sense of meaning. Why are we here? What is the purpose of our existence? The answers change with each generation, but the questions are eternal."[2]

In his book, The Body, Being Light In Darkness, Charles Colson, using an anecdote from the grim days of World War II when the British were trapped in Dunkirk, "During that agonizing period, it is said that the British soldiers broadcast a terse message across the English Channel--just three words--'and if not'. Was that code? No, it was a reference to the Old Testament episode when Shadrach, Meshack, and Abednego stood before the fiery furnace and said, "Our God is able to save us, and He will save us--and if not--we will remain faithful to Him anyway."[3]

In man's most desperate hour, he knows that only God can make a difference. So what is of real importance to each of us seems to be those age-old questions: Where is God? What can I know about eternal life, and how can I insure that I have it? So we feel justified in our lifelong search to find answers to these questions related to our spirituality.

For those of us who have chosen Christianity, we did not leave our inquiring, intelligent minds behind when we placed our faith in Jesus Christ. Quite the contrary, for as we research and study, we find that our faith is built on the strongest kind of evidence that Jesus Christ was heralded by 456 prophesies in the Old Testament.

In historically accepted documentation, Jesus fulfilled the eight categories of these prophesies at a ratio probability of 1 in 100,000,000,000,000,000, according to the probability calculations of one in ten to the 17th power (See the Appendix for a sample of the Prophesies and verifications of the Fulfillments of some of these prophesies made over a period of 1000 years, the latest of which was recorded over 200 years before its fulfillment in Jesus's coming).

"When we do not have sufficient knowledge of why we believe what we believe, we give the impression that our faith is a religion based merely on blind faith or emotional prejudice. Nothing can be further from the truth. We accuse persons who reject our faith, without at least examining the evidence for it, as being prejudiced. Then is it not also true that to accept a faith without examining its evidence is nothing more than credulity and prejudice? Also, when we do not examine the foundations of our faith, Satan can use our ignorance to attack our belief, and then when we experience difficulties, he sows convincing doubt in our minds."[4]

So many have only the most simple knowledge, and only an "early childhood" impression of Jesus Christ; so, therefore, the need to examine Him afresh with an open mind, for his teachings have such a relevance for each of our lives that we are challenged to respond to the same question that Pilate had to answer about the greatest person in recorded history, "What do I do with Jesus?"[5]

Sir Frederick Kenyon of the British Museum, one of the great scholars of our time, points to the fact that archeology has confirmed the scriptures and he agrees with Nelson Glueck, the renowned Jewish archeologist who said, "It may be stated categorically that no archeology discovery has ever controverted a biblical reference, and historical memory of the Bible is almost incredibly accurate, particularly when we see that it is fortified by historical fact."[6]

An American historian, J. Gilchrist Lawson, said, "The legendary or mythical theory of Christ's existence is not held by anyone worthy of the name of scholar. The historical evidences of Christ's existence are so much greater than those in support of any other event in ancient history, for instance, better documented than Napoleon's defeat at Waterloo. No candid scholar could reject them without also renouncing his belief in every event recorded in ancient history."[7]

Most persons suppose that other than the Gospels, no veritable ancient writers wrote about Jesus Christ. They are quite wrong. I have discovered since I set out to see what writers of antiquity and of recent date--secular historians, intellectuals, theologians, cynics, politicians, and literary writers of note through the ages--have said about Jesus, I find the number of references reads like a "Who's Who" of the ages.

Through the years I have met, worked with, and often become friends with persons of varied religious beliefs--with agnostics and with a few atheists. Through these interactions, I have come to agree with Dr. Harry Emerson Fosdick who said, "Some men, often precocious, clever ones, are biased against religion because in youth they accepted an immature philosophy of life and have never changed it. The crust forms too soon on some minds. And if it forms during the period of youthful revolt, they are definitely prejudiced against religious truths. The difference between such folk and the great believers is not that the believers had no doubts, but that they did not fix their final thoughts of life until more mature experience had come."[8]

As Dr. Phillip Schoff of the Yale Divinity School predicted, "I have found that as these persons truly searched and made honest inquiry, if they honestly love and respect truth, even the earnest skeptics will not refuse to accept truth when documented evidence is laid before them."[9]

4

When I became a Christian at the age of 12, I accepted the minister's explanation that because I believed that Jesus Christ is God's son and had asked Him for forgiveness for my sins that Jesus had already paid for all the sins I had or ever would commit. I understood that my responsibility was to try to live for Him and to daily ask for His direction in my life and to always ask for forgiveness for any sins that I committed.

That explanation was sufficient for the time being. But as I matured and began to read and study the Scriptures, the following concerns were unclear and, therefore, troubling to me:

How did Jesus Christ's death occur, and why was it necessary?
What is the significance of His death and the New Covenant to all mankind?
What verification do we have of the authenticity of the New Testament writings?
What have the learned men of all ages said about Jesus?

For my own spiritual growth and for a true understanding of these great questions, I have studied the basic tenets of many of the world's major religions. I have compared them objectively with the authentic records of Christian history and teachings. I have explored the writings of numerous historians, intellectuals, skeptics, politicians, of believers and non-believers, from about 300 B.C. to the present.

I find that the historical evidence for the authenticity of Jesus's life, activities, and His miracles during His three years of ministry is overwhelming. No one who truly searches these resources can disbelieve in Jesus Christ's deity because of lack of evidence.

Hence, Everyman, like Pilate, must make a decision--
"What do I do with Jesus?"

The following pages share the truths I have found in my personal pilgrimage to find answers for these four questions.

# REFERENCES FOR INTRODUCTION

1.  Boyer, Paul. <u>When Time Shall Be No More</u>, Harvard University Press, Cambridge, Massachusetts, September 1972.

2.  White, Gale. "The End is Near," Atlanta Journal and Constitution, Section D, 1/21/96.

3.  Colson, Charles. <u>The Body, Being Light in Darkness</u>, Word Books, Nashville, Tennessee, September 1972.

4.  Kennedy, Dr. James. <u>Why I Believe</u>, World Book Publishing, Waco, Texas, 1981, p. 14.

5.  Green, Michael. <u>Who Is This Jesus</u>, Oliver Nelson, a division of Thomas Nelson Publishing, Nashville, Tennessee, 1992, pp. 6-7.

6.  Kennedy, Dr. James. op. cit., p. 36.

7.  Lawson, J. Gilchrist. <u>Greatest Thoughts About Jesus Christ</u>, Richard K. Smith Company, New York, 1919, p. 160.

8.  Fosdick, Harry Emerson. "A Thought for a New Year," a brochure - no publisher listed.

9.  Schaff, Phillip. "Testimonies of Unbelievers," The American Tract Society, 1865, p. 281.

# SECTION I

# HOW AND WHY JESUS'S DEATH OCCURRED: ITS RELATIONSHIP TO THE NEW COVENANT

## *Jesus's Actions Misunderstood*

The enormous notoriety that Jesus had received was rocking the fragile peace with Rome and was likely to bring down savage reprisals against the Jewish nation, since He was himself Jewish. The Jewish rulers became particularly concerned when the story of Jesus raising Lazarus from the dead had been verified by numerous witnesses. This was especially troubling because the Sadducees did not believe in resurrection. Their hope for a strong man to come and restore their nation to the glory days of David and Solomon, where they could throw off the Roman yoke, was now threatened seriously.[1] In addition, Jesus had been enraged when He entered the temple and saw the rampant buying and selling as if this holy house was a street market. So He defied the temple authorities by driving out the money changers and purging the temple of such commercial corruption.

Most experts agree that His action made His execution highly predictable because as Jerome Nercy of the Weston School of Theology in Boston said, "It was like attacking the Bank of America today,"[2] so the authorities became intent on revenge.

According to N. T. Wright, the Oxford scholar, Jesus's message was revolutionary for He "turned the widespread hope of political salvation into a message of spiritual deliverance."[3] Also, the thinking that a system of laws and rules obeyed could earn salvation and eternal life was now questioned, because many were believing that they were following God's will by having their sins blotted out by Jesus's act of divine amnesty and mercy.

## *Prophesy of New Covenant*

God's covenant made with Israel had included laws about their behavior towards Him and each other, which they were obliged to obey. Yet they had drifted from such responsibility and profaned God's name. "God could lower His standards or change their

11

hearts. The Prophets Ezekiel and Jeremiah had prophesied that He would keep His covenant agreement, but would empower them to keep their side of the bargain by giving them a new heart and put His spirit within them and move them to follow His leading,"[4] and this is what Christ came to do.

When we review the historical actions taken regarding Jesus, it is clear that the Jewish leaders did not themselves crucify Him, but their ruling body did condemn Him to death and sent Him back for the second time to Pilate, the Roman authority, under whose jurisdiction they acted.

### Roman Record of Jesus's Trial

According to Roman government records, Jesus's trial was conducted in three stages:

I.  Annas, the father-in-law of Caiphas the official high priest, conducted the preliminary examination of Jesus which apparently had two objectives--

    First, by asking about Jesus's followers, as trainees to lead a revolt against the Roman government; and

    Second, to gather evidence that Jesus had been teaching heresy.

    Jesus declared that He had nothing to hide, that He taught openly, and that people came to the synagogue and elsewhere to hear Him on their own volition. Since ample witnesses were available to give first-hand accounts of His teachings, Jesus suggested that a better course of action was to call such persons to testify. Actually, requiring Jesus to testify against himself was a violation of Roman law.[5]

    Annas, unable to secure sufficient evidence, sent Jesus, bound, on to Caiphas, who as high priest presided over the Sanhedrin (the supreme Jewish body made up of chief priests, elders, and scribes).

II. After being condemned by the Sanhedrin, Jesus was taken to Pilate's headquarters. Pilate went outside to meet the Jews because they would not go inside for fear of becoming ritually unclean through contact with Gentiles at Passover. Pilate directed that since Jesus was Jewish that the Jews must judge Him, so He was returned for the second time for trial before the Sanhedrin. Shortly before dawn, the Sanhedrin returned Jesus, condemned, to Pilate, saying that they could not execute Him themselves because by law only the Roman government could do so.

III. Pilate questioned Him again and was convinced that He had done nothing worthy of death, saying he felt Jesus had no political ambitions; however, as the Roman official he had investigated the matter because Jesus's own people had brought the charges. In legal terms, people are tried for what they have done; in Jesus's case, He was tried for who He was.

Pilate then attempted to release Him, appealing to the custom of releasing a prisoner at Passover. The Jews then threatened that Pilate would be considered an enemy of Caesar if he released a man who claimed to be King. So Pilate knowing that he was trapped if he overlooked an act of treason sarcastically presented Jesus as their King, asking, "Shall I crucify your king?" The chief priest declared that they had no king but Caesar.

Pilate then disregarded his wife's caution and, in an attempt to declare himself innocent, ceremoniously washed his hands publicly and with the authority of his office delivered Jesus to the Passover crowd to be crucified.[6]

## *Crucifiction and Burial of Jesus*

Under the most extreme circumstances to be imagined, Jesus, hanging on the cross and jeered by the crowd saying, "Save yourself if you are God's son," exhibited a trait that is beyond human comprehension. He spoke to God saying, "Father, forgive them for they know not what they are doing."

Jesus's death was verified by the Roman soldiers at the scene by piercing His side with a sword, and following the prophesy in Psalms 34:30, His legs were not broken as was the custom because it was evident that He was already dead.

The feeble belief that He had merely swooned was thoroughly discounted, according to testimony of the Roman centurion sent by Pilate to verify His death by piercing His side with a spear producing both blood and water--empirical evidence that life had ceased because blood had separated into its constituent elements--as reported in the official Roman record.[7]

"Archaeological discoveries and textual research in recent years have added considerable weight to the Gospel accounts. Found among the Dead Sea Scrolls, for example, was a Temple document; scholars say the text suggests that the Law of Moses may have been understood in Jesus's time to prescribe crucifixion in certain cases. The German theologian, Ernst Bammel, has noted that execution by crucifixion had been used in Palestine since the second century B.C.--even by Jewish courts. Because it was a particularly gruesome form of punishment, said Bammel, 'it was used especially in political cases such as those branded by the Romans as rebellion.'

"Striking corroboration of the type of crucifixion that is described in the Gospels was discovered in 1968 at an excavation site near Mount Scopus, just northeast of Jerusalem. Three tombs were found on the site, one of them containing the remains of a man who had been crucified between A.D. 7 and 70. The man's feet had been nailed together at the heels, his forearms had nail wounds and the bones of his lower legs had been broken--wounds that are entirely consistent with the description of John's Gospel of the crucifixion of Jesus and the two thieves, except that Jesus's legs were not broken.

"Using computer models, astronomers have ruled out a solar eclipse in Palestine at that time. And while they say a lunar eclipse did occur on April 3 in A.D. 33, it could not have been seen in Jerusalem during the daylight hours."[8]

Jesus was crucified during Passover when a full moon was in evidence. Astronomers tell us that there cannot be a solar eclipse during a full moon, so the darkness that covered the earth for three hours has no possible scientific explanation.

According to the Jewish custom of that time, the whole body, including the head, was wrapped in grave clothes, with a hundred pounds of spices between the folds and filling the body orifices.[9] After the corpse was placed in a borrowed tomb, a huge stone closed the opening, the Romans' seal was affixed, and Roman guards were placed on 24-hour vigils, with the routine threat of death if they relinquished their vigilance.[10]

## The Resurrection

When on the third day the tomb was verified as empty and when the guards who had fled were found, they were directed by the Sanhedrin to say that the disciples had stolen the body while they were asleep. As Dr. F. F. Bruce, Rylands Professor of Biblical Criticism at the University of Manchester, stated, "As you know, the presence of hostile witnesses serves as further evidence of an occurrence of an event."[11] So the empty tomb was accepted as empty by Jewish leaders who had convicted Him, for the verified news was too notorious to be denied.

## Social Consequences of Resurrection

Dr. Paul Althaus comments: "The resurrection could not have been maintained in Jerusalem for a single day, for a single hour, if the empty tomb had not been established as a fact for all concerned."[12]

Dr. Paul L. Maier concludes: "If all the evidence is weighed carefully and fairly, it is indeed justifiable, according to the canons of historical research, to conclude that the tomb in which Jesus was buried was actually empty on the third day after his crucifixion. And no shred of evidence has yet been discovered in literary sources, epigraphy, or archaeology that would disprove this statement."[13]

Regarding the theory advanced by the Sanhedrin that the disciples had stolen the body while the guards slept, J.N.D. Anderson, Dean of the Faculty of Law at the University of London, says, "The depression and cowardice exhibited by the disciples during the trial and crucifixion of Jesus provide a hard-hitting argument against their suddenly becoming so brave and daring as to face a detachment of Roman soldiers at the tomb and attempt to take the corpse when they were, of course, unarmed. Furthermore, it would not begin to explain their dramatic transformation from dejected and dispirited escapists into witnesses whom no opposition could muzzle after they realized that Jesus had arisen." They were the first to hear the trumpet of hope that has echoed down through the centuries in every cemetary of the world that makes the experience of death not a bitter end, but the dawning of a new phase of life, for Jesus said, "I am the resurrection and the life: he that believeth in me, though he were dead, yet shall he live."[14]

The situation at the tomb is significant. The Roman seal was broken which meant automatic crucifixion upside down for those who did it. Justin, in his Digest 49-16, lists 18 offenses for which a guard of that period could be put to death. These included falling asleep or leaving one's position unguarded.

According to legal records, in the entire history of jurisprudence, there has never been a witness, under any circumstances, who has been allowed to testify to what transpired while he himself was asleep.[15]

In reality, one has to question--if Jesus had merely swooned as some cynics propose and had come to following his severe injuries-- how could He have rolled the heavy stone up the hill and escaped? In addition, how could He have walked the 14 miles to Emmaus and back on pierced feet?[16]

### Shroud of Turin Researched

The Shroud of Turin, now in the museum in Turin, Italy, has been of question since the days of the Crusaders as to its authenticity of being the cloak worn by Jesus at the time of His trial. The one carbon 14 test attempted did not prove its exactness, and the fragile condition of the garment discourages researchers duplicate testing. However, the pathologist's report indicates the following:

- the garment is made of flax;
- the garment contains a pollen found only in the Middle East;
- it shows a facial image characteristic of the Jewish ethnic group;
- it indicates that the person wearing it had had a flogging type of experience due to the amount and placement of the blood stains;
- it is specifically shown that the wearer suffered a pierced arm and a knee injury;
- the image is identified as caused by a type of radiation (reflections by scientists who are also Christians indicate that God employed a radiation-type resurrection process).[17]

## Jesus's Teaching Process

Professional educators throughout the centuries, since Socrates, have known that teaching is not "telling." The Socratic method of teaching, beginning in the third century B. C., whereby one's thought is provoked in the exploration of truth, rather than being provided facts and a strict set of rules and laws to be followed without alternatives, had not been accepted by the Israeli world. Jesus, instead, stressed the pursuit of truth by the process of prayer, asking God's direction of thought and action, giving such direction as, "Seek and you shall find," rather than, "Let me tell you and you will know." So, because the activity of individually seeking spiritual truth and knowledge was not pushed by the prevalent religion, one might say that the failure of the Israeli intelligentsia to recognize the fulfillment of the prophesies of their own forbearers in the life and work of Jesus is simply, but realistically, expressed in the words of the Negro spiritual, "Poor Little Jesus Boy, They Didn't Know Who You Wuz."

## Why Jesus's Blood Required for Atonement

After years of research of the scriptures and the writings of many learned scholars and theologians, I have an understanding and acceptance of the need for Christ's death.

Since Adam and Eve sinned and were expelled from the Garden of Eden, there had been no atonement except through the blood of lambs sprinkled on the alter by a priest, as described in Leviticus 16, because the Scriptures teach that without the shedding of blood there is no forgiveness. That is the reason that every culture practices some form of blood atonement, as the word atonement means to cover.

In each case the lamb must be killed for its blood to be shed, so that explains why Jesus willingly made an <u>eternal atonement</u> for our sins in His death, by giving his life's blood not on an alter, but on a cross. His death, as the <u>Son of God</u>, eliminated the penalty then that prevented God from giving us forgiveness and the eternal life that He wanted to give mankind, ever since the beginning.

In a Red Cross office, in a little box, were brochures entitled, "A Gift of Blood," lettered in red. They serve as a challenge to people to assist with the blood program, for blood means the difference between life and death for ill patients. Blood represents life as in Leviticus 17:11, "For the life of the flesh is in the blood, and I have given it to you on the altar as an atonement for your soul." The blood sacrifice runs throughout the Old Testament--a foreshadowing or a symbol of Christ's sacrifice. Christ's death on the cross brings man out from under the law of Moses. The law condemns man, but Jesus justified that claim. There is no possible way to escape the final judgment of Almighty God but to identify with the Christ of the cross who has paid the atonement price with his own blood.[18]

So apart from that blood given in exchange for a life, there is no true cleansing of sin and no conquest of death by grace giving life eternal. Jesus also took away the fear of death by taking away the fear of judgment because He had made our atonement in His once-for-all sacrifice--not by an animal's blood, but by His own life's blood. God's plan requires our placing our faith in Jesus Christ and accepting His free gift; then our sins are forgiven upon our individual request, and we enter into a new relationship with God.[19]

### Decision by Faith Brings Grace

This was different from the religious thought of that time and is referred to by some current religions today as too good to be true.

Thomas Chalmers and John Knox, great scholars and theologians from Scotland, wrote:

> "Not by works, but by grace
> are we saved through faith--
> a gift from God.
> Not rich enough to buy it,
> Not erudite enough to learn or earn it.
> Not strong enough to win it.
> Our works not good enough to deserve it.
> All it takes then is to believe
> God's Son's promise."[20]

This belief is so ably expressed by John Newton, the ex-slave trader who wrote the hymn, "Amazing Grace," after he accepted God's gracious forgiveness following a life of deep degradation.

We are never brought into the right relationship with God by joining a church, synagogue, or temple, nor through a group experience. No minister, priest, rabbi, parent, or religious leader can communicate the decision for us. We must establish our own relationship by individually communicating to God that we accept the penance Christ paid for us and we submit the guidance of our life to His direction. Just as in the case of the blood of the Passover on the black night of the death angel in the land of Egypt, each male child was <u>individually</u> saved by the sacrificial blood.[21]

### God's First Two Covenants

The first recorded covenant of God with man was consummated with Noah and the promise that He would not destroy man again with a flood, and He sealed the covenant with the rainbow. The second covenant was with Abraham with the promise that He would be the God of the Israelites and that they would be His people: that promise was ratified with the rite of circumcision.

Jeremiah prophesied 600 years later, as recorded in Jeremiah 31:31-34 and in 32:40 that God would make a new covenant with man in the days to come to replace the one made with the Exodus generation. That ancient covenant made the divine will plain to them, but <u>did not</u> impart the power to carry it out, and so for lack of power they broke the covenant. Through clarification of the difference in the two first covenants and the New Covenant, we can better understand why the Israelites continuously broke the ancient covenant. God's will, ratified by the blood of sacrificial animals was made plain to them, but they lacked the power of the Holy Spirit to carry out His will.

### The New Covenant

When Jesus, the night before His death, interpreted the meaning of the everlasting New Covenant, as predicted by Jeremiah, He explained that not only the desire but also the power to do the will of God would be imparted to all believers, because God's law would be put within them and written within their hearts. He explained that the wine offered symbolizes the sacrifice of His, not an animal's, blood and that it not only externally purified from defilement but inwardly cleanses the conscience from guilt. He spoke also of the fulfilling of all of the earlier prophesies in the Old Covenant, particularly of Isaiah 53, which revealed that His New Covenant would give an amnesty to all. He explained that when He ascended to His Father that He would leave the Holy Spirit within the heart of all believers to enable them to overcome the evil they would encounter.[22]

This was actually a substantiation of what He said when He had initiated His ministry in the Nazareth synagogue three years earlier, by reading from Isaiah 61. He had said on that occasion, "Today this scripture has been fulfilled in your hearing." He read the scriptures from the scrolls of the Hebrew Bible that He had grown up reading in His home synagogue in Nazareth, and they were equally familiar to all of the people in attendance.[23]

In the New Covenant, no one nation was selected. "There is neither Jew nor Greek; there is neither slave nor free; there is neither male nor female, for you are all one in Christ Jesus." Jesus intended to call all people out of a divided world and weld them together, in love, to become the nucleus of a new called and chosen people. His followers would become a new model nation to represent God's way of life that leads to peace and salvation. Under the New Covenant, all humanity becomes the chosen people. Jesus thus showed that the new spiritual Israel would not be limited to the physical descendants of the Old Testament chosen people. As the church began to expand to the Gentile world, and people from all varied backgrounds were called and converted, Christianity struck at the roots of prejudice. Jews, Gentiles, slaves, men, women, and the rich and famous soon found themselves united in a new relationship with God and with one another.

### Justification

Justification is a metaphor borrowed from the court room to define a declaration that goes beyond guilty or innocent. There is then not a case to judge, as the person is considered to be in the right. But we know that no human being is righteous. As Paul wrote, "The righteousness of Jesus Christ must be given, or imputed to us; therefore, if His righteousness is in us, we are justified."

No human being has the power on his own to meet God's standards of righteousness. But through the Holy Spirit which Jesus gives when one accepts His grace, God fulfills the promise first given through Jeremiah and repeated in the New Testament in Hebrews, "I will put my laws in their mind and write them on their hearts and I will be their God, and they shall be my people."[24]

### Eleventh Commandment

Thus in the New Covenant established by Jesus's sacrificial blood, He added another commandment to the ten, which God had given to man centuries earlier. In the eleventh commandment, He admonishes His followers to love their neighbor and all men and to practice forgiveness in all relationships.

# REFERENCES FOR SECTION I

1. <u>Jewish Encyclopedia</u>. Funk and Wagnall Co., New York, 1906, Volume 8, p. 508.

2. <u>U. S. News and World Report</u>, April 16, 1996, p. 48.

3. Wright, N. T. <u>Jesus and the Victory of God</u>, Oxford University Press, 1995.

   Additional References:

   <u>Time</u>, April 19, 1996, "The Search for Jesus."

   <u>The Plain Truth</u>, "The Gospel: Your Invitation to the Kingdom," 11/94, p. 15.

4. Lamb, Jonathan. "United in the Holy Spirit." Decision. (June 1995), Billy Graham Association.

5. McDowell, Josh. <u>More Than A Carpenter</u>. Living Book Series, Lyndale Pub., Wheaton, Illinois, 1973, pp. 21-23.

6. Stephens, Shirley. "Jesus Trial." <u>Bible Book Study for Adults</u>, Southern Baptist Pub., Nashville, Tennessee, 1994, pp. 71-82.

7. McDowell, op. cit., pp. 94 and 97.

   Kennedy, James. <u>Why I Believe the Bible</u>. Word Bks. Pub., Waco, Texas, 1981, p. 115.

8. <u>U. S. News and World Report</u>, April 19, 1996, p. 48.

9. McDowell, op. cit., pp. 90-91.

10. Ibid, p. 92.

11. Bruce, F. F. <u>Archeological Confirmation of the New Testament in Revolution and the Bible</u>. Baker Book House, Grand Rapids, 1969, p. 331.

Anderson, Robert. The Lord From Heaven. James Nisbet and Company, Ltd., London, 1910, p. 5.

12. Altheus, Paul. Die Wahrheit des kirch lichin Osterglaubens (gutersloh C. Bertels mann) 1941, pp. 222 and 225.

13. McDowell, Josh. Evidence that Demands a Verdict. Campus Crusade for Christ International, 1973, p. 231.

14. Anderson, J. N. D. Christianity: The Witness of History. Tyndale Press, 1976, p. 92.

15. Kennedy, James. Why I Believe the Bible. Word Books Pub., Waco, Texas, 1981, p. 111.

16. Ibid, p. 116.

17. Television program on Arts and Entertainment Channel in Ancient Mysteries Series, Spring 1994.

18. Graham, Billy. "Death the Enemy." Decision, September 1975, p. 12, Billy Graham Association, Minneapolis, Minnesota.

19. Ibid.

20. Ibid.

21. Stephens, Shirley. (Same as in Ref. 6), p. 82.

22. Bruce, F. F. The Canon of Scripture. Intervarsity Press, Downers Grove, Illinois, 1988, pp. 20-21.

23. Graham, Billy. Decision, June 1995, p. 26.

24. The Plain Truth, October 1992, p. 6.

# SECTION II

# THE AUTHENTICITY OF THE NEW TESTAMENT

The New Testament is the main source of information concerning the influential life that Christ lived. Scholars generally agreed that the four gospels, written mainly in Greek, were recorded within 40 to 60 years of Christ's death on the cross.[1] Why did these inspired disciples not immediately write full descriptions of Christ's life, miracles, teachings, and resurrection?

*The Disciples' Actions*

The disciples did not wait 50 or 60 years to proclaim that Jesus had risen when no one was around to deny it. They proclaimed it orally immediately, though they were threatened and flogged, imprisoned, and later even put to death for proclaiming the truth they had witnessed. Christ's death and resurrection was an open book. No one could deny that the tomb was empty. Even the soldiers and the ruling authorities admitted that. But the empty tomb alone was not what convinced the disciples that Jesus was alive; it was His personal appearance for 40 days that provided the infallible truth. At least 500 people saw Him alive--in outside appearances, walking, eating, and many even touched Him, according to Paul's writings. All that the authorities needed to do was to open the tomb and show that the corpse was still there and identify the person appearing to be Jesus as an imposter. They could not produce the corpse, and in their uncertainty and fear, they propagated the swoon myth and accused his followers of theft.[2]

*Eyewitness Verification*

It is known that the native language of the disciples was Aramaic, the language of Palestine. Aramaic was characterized by a rhyming cadence, and since Jews--and the disciples were mainly of Jewish descent--learned by memory, the rhyming cadence used by Jesus in His teaching made it easy to commit to memory His actual words. Following Pentecost, these men were so transformed from timid cowards to brave proclaimers who now spoke in other tongues, that they attracted streams of new converts, which kept them too busy to write until later. Then, perhaps, they felt that many of the eye witnesses were dying out. One of the strong points of their writings is the confidential appeal to the knowledge of the hearers, for they not only said, "We are witnesses of these things," but also added, "As you yourselves know." The presence of living witnesses would have served as a corrective.

So the disciples finally realized that if they were to follow Jesus's final admonition to spread the gospel throughout the world, they must write their testimony as eye witnesses to insure continuity of their beliefs and witness of what they could verify had happened.[3]

## The Septuagint and Early Writings

We know that by that time, the Jewish, Greco-Roman world preferred the written to the spoken word because of the Septuagint, which had occurred around 200 B.C. At that time, 72 elders of Israel were brought to Alexandria with their own Hebrew scrolls from the Israeli synagogues for the purpose of translating the first five books of the Old Testament into Greek for the benefit of the large Jewish element which had settled in Alexandria soon after it was founded by Alexander the Great. The term, Septuagint (Latin for 70) came to be attached to the work of the group because the elders completed the translation in 72 days, achieving an agreed upon version on final comparison. Their work was so inspired, according to a document called the Letter of Aristeas, that such a common translation was accomplished even though the elders were isolated from one another in separate cells, they nevertheless produced the same text. So from that time forward, it is noted that the Greek translation became an accepted language to the Jews because they felt that God was responsible for the Septuagint.[4]

No ancient documents in the world come down to us with such a wealth of manuscript tradition as the gospels. We have copies that go back to within a century of their composition, which is incredible compared with the classical authors of the period.

Discovery of the John Ryland Papyri manuscripts, A. D. 130, and the Chester Beatty Papyri, A. D. 155, have increased scholarly confidence that every book of the New Testament was written by baptized Jews between the 40s and 80s or 90s of the first century, according to Sir William Ramsey and William Allbright, two of the world's foremost biblical archeologists.[6]

## Credibility of the Gospels

No books in all of the world's literature have been subjected to such thorough and persistent scrutiny over a period of hundreds of years as have the Gospels. Today, their credibility stands as high as ever because they emerge from every test with the utmost credit because they meet every criteria using the most critical tools of Bible scholars, according to Dr. Clark Pinnock, professor of systemic theology at Regents College.[7] He agrees with A. N. Sherwin-White, the classical historian who confirms the historicity of the New Testament saying, "Any attempt to reject its basic historicity must now appear absurd. Roman historians have long taken it for granted."[8] He continues to discuss the problem on the part of many in applying one standard or test to secular literature and another to the Bible. He insists on applying the same tests to all literature, whether secular or religious.

## Criterion of Multiple Attestation

Three of the most simple are the Criterion of Multiple Attestation, which means that there is added reason to accept the authenticity of an event or saying if it is recorded in more than one place, by a different author.[9]

## Historian's Reliability Tests

Another tool, for the linguist, is the matter of Aramaic, the language of Palestine in Jesus's day and that which he usually spoke. Aramaic experts find that the teachings of Jesus can be easily translated back into the underlying Aramaic, and as a result they fall into the rhyming cadences used by the Jews of that time.

Thirdly, the uniqueness of the Gospels fits the secular evidence from the non-Christian historians who refer to the fact that parables were not used before nor after Jesus's teachings.[10]

In keeping with Pinnock's and Sherwin-White's belief regarding historical reliability testing by the same process that all historical documents are tested. Military historian, C. Sanders used the three basic principals of historiography:[11]

> Bibliographical Test--an examination of the textual transmission by which documents reach us.

The history of Thucydides (460-400 B.C.), available about 1700 A.D., 1300 years after he wrote it, is accepted by classical scholars as authentic.

Aristotle wrote his poetics around 343 B.C., and the earliest copy we have is dated 1100 A.D. Caesar composed his history of the Gallic Wars 58-60 B.C., and its manuscript authority rests on nine copies dating 1000 years after his death.

So, when it comes to the manuscript of the New Testament, the abundance of material is almost embarrassing in contrast. Sir Frederick Kenyon, Director and Principal Librarian of the British Museum, and second to none in authority in issuing statements about manuscripts says, "The interval then between the dates of the original composition and the earliest extant evidence becomes so small as to be in fact negligible, and the last foundation for any doubt that the scriptures have come down to us substantially as they were written has now been removed. Both the authenticity and the general integrity of the books of the New Testament may be regarded as finally established."[12]

Internal Evidence Test is the process following Aristotle's dictum: "The benefit of the doubt is to be given to the document itself."

Dr. Louis Gottschalk, former history professor at the University of Chicago, points out that the ability of the writer to tell the truth is important to the historian in his determination of credibility. He identifies the fact that the ability to tell the truth is closely related to the witness's nearness, both geographically and chronologically to the events recorded.[13]

Will Durant, who was trained in the discipline of historical investigation said, "Despite the prejudices and inexperience of the disciples, they record many incidents that mere inventors would not have revealed, for instance, the doubts of Thomas, Peter's denial, and the competition of the apostles for high places in the Kingdom."[14]

We see that New Testament writers were hard on even their heroes. Who in the early church would have written such things about prominent church leaders unless those things were literally true?

<u>External Evidence Test</u> is the test of whether other historical material confirms or denies the internal testimony of the documents.

Gottschalk says that conformity or agreement with other known historical or scientific facts is often the decisive test of evidence.[15]

Two friends of the Apostle John confirm the internal evidence from John's accounts. The Apostle John, himself, used to say, "Mark having been the interpreter of Peter, wrote down accurately all that Peter mentioned, whether sayings or doings of Christ.

Irenaeus, Bishop of Lyons (A.D. 180), was a student of Polycarp, Bishop of Smyrna, who had been a Christian for 86 years and was a disciple of John the Apostle, wrote, "Matthew published his Gospel among the Hebrew Jews in their own tongue, while Peter and Paul were preaching in Rome and founding churches there. Luke, the follower of Paul, set down in a book the gospel preached by Paul after he and Peter were crucified in Rome during the reign of Nero." He goes on to verify the vision John had on the Isle of Patmos when Christ appeared to him revealing truths of that and of future times and gave John the direction to, "Write what you have seen. Write what is now and what will take place later."[16]

## Evidence of New Covenant's Effect

If one has difficulty believing the power and strength of the New Covenant, he has but to look at the amazing change in the eleven apostles. All of these men came from the middle or lower socioeconomic strata. They were generally uneducated, ambivalent, generally uninspired. But as Jesus promised, the Holy Spirit descended upon them each at Pentecost, changing them to inspired, knowledgeable, jubilant speakers who could command attention because they suddenly could communicate in the numerous languages of their day. They were suddenly unafraid to speak of the significance of the life and death of Jesus, whom they identified as God's Son, the Promised Messiah, in the synagogues, on the streets, market places, and wherever they found people to listen.

God's favor was evident in His support of the spread of the Christian movement as Christian churches began to be developed throughout the known world of that time, from Asia to Europe, according to the missionary writings of the Apostles, and the political journals of that period. Interestingly, God's support of the Christian movement was evident in the fact that He had allowed tremendous networks of transportation and communication to be explored and set up by Marco Polo, Alexander the Great, and in the organization of the Roman Empire.

## *Disciples' Dedication*

Men do not willingly give their lives for something they are not absolutely sure is true.[17] And so because of their belief in the New Covenant given to the world by Jesus Christ, and in response to the Holy Spirit within their hearts, 12 of the major followers of Jesus were tortured, flogged, imprisoned, and then finally faced death by some of the cruelest methods then known:

Peter - crucified upside down on a rough wooden cross;
James (brother of John) - beheaded by King Agrippa;
Mark - dragged through the streets of Alexandria and then burned;
Paul - beheaded by a Roman sword (at Nero's command);
Andrew - crucified;
Phillip - crucified;
Simon - crucified;
Bartholemew - crucified;

32

James (son of Alphaeus) - crucified;
Matthew - killed by sword thrust;
James (son of Zebedee) - killed by sword thrust;
Thomas - killed by a spear thrust;
Thaddaeus - killed by arrows;
James (brother of Jesus) - stoned to death.

The only surviving apostle was John, who experienced all of the same inhumane atrocities as the other martyrs except death. He died of natural causes in Ephesus after writing his epistle and the Book of the Revelation.[18]

The steadfastness of these apostles even to death cannot be explained away, for as Harold Mattingly in his history text on Roman civilization writes, "The apostles sealed their witness with their life's blood."[19]

## *Legal Verification*

Dr. Simon Greenleaf, one of the greatest legal minds ever produced and who was lauded by H. W. H. Knotts in the <u>Dictionary of American Biography</u> as the person mainly responsible for the rise of the Harvard Law School to its eminent position, examined the legal value of the testimony of the resurrection of Christ. He observed that it was impossible that the disciples would have persisted in their testimony to death had not Jesus actually risen from the dead, and had they not known this fact as certainly as they knew any other fact.

Greenleaf, who wrote three volumes on methods of determining legal evidence and who lectured for years on how to break down a witness and determine whether or not he is lying, concluded, "The apostles had every possible motive to review carefully the grounds of their faith and the evidence they supported; and so I conclude that the resurrection of Jesus Christ is one of the best supported events in human history, according to the laws of legal evidence administered in courts of justice anywhere in the world."[20]

# REFERENCES FOR SECTION II

1. Wilson, Rev. Jerre. North Peachtree Messenger, April 9, 1995, p. 8.

2. Ibid.

3. Ibid.

4. Bruce, F. F. The Canon of Scripture. Intervarsity Press, Downers Grove, Illinois, 1988.

5. McDowell, Josh. More Than A Carpenter. Living Books, Tyndale House Pub., Inc., Wheaton, Illinois, 1973.

6. Albright, Wm F. From the Stone Age to Christianity (Second Edition). John Hopkins Press, Baltimore, Maryland, 1946, pp. 297-298.

   Ramsey, Wm. The Bearing of Recent Discovery in Bible Lands. Funk and Wagnalls, New York, 1955, p. 136.

7. Pinnock, Dr. Clark. Set Forth Your Case. Craig Press, 1968, p. 58.

8. Sherwin-White, A. N. Roman Society and Roman Law in the New Testament. Clarendon Press, Oxford, 1963, p. 189.

9. Gottschalk, Louis R. Understanding History. Knapf Pub., New York, 1969, p. 150.

10. Green, Michael. Who Is This Jesus? Thomas Nelson Pub., Nashville, Tennessee, 1992, pp. 131-132.

11. Sanders, C. Introduction to Research in English Literary History. McMillan Pub., New York, 1952, p. 143.

12. Kenyon, Sir Frederick. <u>The Bible and Archeology</u>. Harper and Rowe Pub., New York, 1940, pp. 288-289.

13. Gottchalk, Ibid.

14. Durant, Will. <u>Caesar and Christ in the Story of Civilization</u> (Volume 3) Simon and Shuster Pub., New York, 1963, p. 557.

15. Gottchalk, op. cit., p. 161.

16. Irenaeus. <u>Against Heresies</u>. 3-1-1. Quoted also in McDowell listed above, p. 56.

17. McDowell, op. cit., p. 60.

18. McDowell, op. cit., p. 61.

19. Mattingly, Harold. <u>Roman Imperial Civilization</u>. Edward Arnold Pub., London, 1967, p. 226.

20. Greenleaf, Dr. Simon. <u>An Examination of the Testimony of the Four Evangelists by the Rules of Evidence Administered in the Courts of Justice</u>. Boher Book House, Grand Rapids, 1965. (Reprint of 1874 Edition, Cockroft and Company, New York, 1874.)

# SECTION III

# LEARNED MEN'S DECISIONS ABOUT JESUS

Everyman since 33 A.D. has dealt with the same question posed by Pontius Pilate, "What will I do with this man Jesus?"--a one-of-a-kind individual--humble, yet authoritative; a winsome martyr from whose birth date the world's time line has been reckoned.

Everyman--from the bush dweller of Central Sudan and the aborigine from the Outback to the philosophic geniuses of the ages, from the princes to the paupers, even the most powerful military and political rulers and the greatest literary figures, to your neighbor, the man on the street--and to each of us--has a decision to make regarding this 2064-year-old question.

It has strengthened and substantiated my faith to review the thoughts of a sample of these noted publics through the ages.

*Earliest Writings About Jesus*

Other than the apostles, Pontius Pilate, whose long report was found in the Caesar archives in Rome, described the miracles of Christ:

> "And Herod, Archelaus and Phillip Annas and Caiphas, with all the people, delivered him to me, making a great uproar against me that I should try him. I therefore ordered him to be crucified, having first scourged him, but having found against him no cause of evil accusations or deeds. And at the time he was crucified, there was darkness over all the world; the sun being darkened at mid-day, and the stars appearing, but in them there appeared no luster; and the moon, as if turned into blood, failed in her light."[1]

A secular writer, Thallus, a Samaritan who wrote in 52 A.D., regarded the crucifixion of Jesus so significant that he included it in his history of the world, and he attempted to explain the darkness that fell on the earth at mid-day as an eclipse of the sun. However, scientists have nullified this theory; for since Passover occurs at the time of a full moon, an eclipse of the sun is not astronomically possible.[2]

In referencing the use of astronomy to discount an eclipse of the sun at the time of the crucifixion, it is revelatory also to consider the significance of the bright star over Bethlehem on the night of Jesus' birth. Cuneiform tablets (the ancient equivalent of newsprint) have turned up in archeological findings in Sippar in Babylonia (the Greenwich of the ancient world), written in 8 B.C. and foretelling the conjunction of Jupiter and Saturn the following year. So in 7 B.C., there was a conjunction between those planets three times in the portion of the sky known as "The Fishes Phenomenon," which happens only once in 794 years. We know that the stars had much meaning to the wise men of that era. Jupiter denoted a world ruler; Saturn was the star of Palestine, and the Fishes indicated the last days. This meant to the sages that the ruler of the world would appear in Palestine soon; therefore, the Wise Men set out to find him. Hence, we see Herod took seriously the threat posed by the male child born at this particular time, especially when he realized that the Wise Men had gone to Bethlehem. No doubt King Herod and the Wise Men knew of the prophesies of Isaiah, Micah, and Jeremiah, for they were learned men of their time.[3]

A Syrian, called Mara bar Serapin, a non-Christian, wrote in 70 A.D. reflecting on his own unfortunate persecution, "What advantage did the Athenians get from putting Socrates to death? Only plague and famine. What advantage did the Jews get from seeing that their wise king was executed? Nothing but the sacking of their city, and the dispersion of their nation." This is an obvious reference not only to Jesus and his death but also to Pilate's sarcastic reference to Jesus as the King of the Jews.[4]

Judaism gives interesting evidence about Jesus. There are allusions to Jesus scattered in the writings of the rabbis, most usually hostile. However, the Jewish guerrilla commander, Flavius Josephus, who led his people in war against Rome between 66 and 70 A.D., subsequently turned historian and tried to improve the reputation of his people in Rome's eyes. He wrote the following concerning Jesus, which is repeated in several of his numerous manuscripts:

"And there arose about this time (he is referring to Pilate's time as governor, A.D. 26-36) Jesus, a wise man, if indeed one should call him a man. For he was a performer of astonishing deeds, a teacher of those who are happy to receive the truth. He won over many Jews and Greeks. He was the Christ (or Messiah). In response to a charge presented by the leading man among us, Pilate condemned him to the cross, but those who loved him did not give up. For he appeared to them on the third day alive again, as the holy prophets had foretold, and had said many wonderful things about him. And still to this day, the race of Christians, named after him, has not died out. (Antiquities, 18.3.3.)"

Dr. William Wheaton of Cambridge University, the best translator today of Josephus' works, regards this as a powerful attestation from a hostile contemporary of Jesus. He surmises that Josephus depended on the Septuagint translation from Palestine sources in referring to the writings of the early prophets regarding the Messiah in his writing of the Antiquities. Josephus later wrote of the work of the apostles and elders in projecting the gospel to the Gentiles who became Christians in the Apostolic Constitution.[5]

Tacitus, a historian who was made governor of Asia in 112 A.D., wrote that Nero and not the Christians was responsible for the burning of much of Rome in 64 A.D., but that he had tried to substitute the Christians as the culprits and had treated them to most extreme punishments. Tacitus referred to the Christians again in his lost book, Histories, of which an excerpt discusses Christ's execution by Pilate, governor of Judea from 26 to 36 A.D., and of the great numbers who became followers of Christianity. In this excerpt he also says that the Roman general, Titus, hoped, by destroying the temple in Jerusalem in 70 A.D., to put an end to both Judaism and Christianity.

A contemporary of Tacitus, Pliny, the Younger who governed Turkey in 112 A.D., wrote of the economic problems caused by the Christians because the pagan temples and festivals were deserted and the demand for sacrificial animals had ceased. But he wrote

Emperor Trajan that he had qualms about his execution of those who practiced Christianity because their lives were exemplary. He stated that one did not find fraud, adultery, theft, or dishonesty among them.[6]

It is fascinating that the only fragment found of the writings of <u>Quadritis</u>, the first Christian apologist, who wrote in 124 A.D. to commend Christianity to the Roman Emperor Hadrian consisted of the following:

> "But the works of the Savior were always present in those who were healed and those who rose from the dead. They were not only seen in the act of being healed while Christ was on earth, but they remained with us after His departure as well."[7]

<u>Julian, the Apostate</u>, wrote a book defying Christianity and went to Jerusalem to disprove the authenticity of the Bible, but he failed, and he finally affirmed the authenticity of the gospels, Matthew, Mark, Luke, and John. However, though he did not realize it, he confirmed the Biblical prophesy by destroying the wall of Babylon. When he came to his death by being wounded on the battlefield, he gathered his blood and threw it into the air and pointing his dagger up to the sky he said, "Thou hast conquered, oh Galilean!"[8]

We know that thousands of slaves, many of whom were Christian believers, were forced to participate in the gladiator fights in the arena in Rome to entertain the perverted Roman mobs.

"One day a Christian named <u>Telemachus</u> leaped into the arena between two gladiators and held them apart. At a sign from the Emperor, he was pierced with their swords. There was no jubilant cry from the mob, for as they looked at this saintly man lying dead in his blood, a silence filled the arena. Quietly and ashamedly the crowd left the stadium and there was never another gladiator show. Telemachus, by sacrificing his life, saved the lives of thousands of others. The blood of such martyrs became the seed of the Christian movement. Later when Constantine, a Christian, was placed on the throne, the mightiest empire the world had seen, collapsed and the influence of the Galilean carpenter began to change a pagan world."[9]

Cyprian, a wealthy noble who lived in the third century, rode around Carthage in a gold chariot, wearing clothes studded with diamonds, living a debauched life. Though he wanted to be like the Christians he saw, he wrote one of the major theologians that he could never give up his inveterate tastes and desires and the sins he so much enjoyed. Following much prayer on the part of many, including himself, he became a true believer. The Holy Spirit, which entered his heart, enabled him to change his whole life and he was transformed into one of the great leaders of the early church.[10]

When at the Last Supper, Jesus foretold of his betrayal and said, "I tell you this now, before it takes place, and when it does, you will believe that I am he, referring to his debate with the Jews about Abraham, when he had said, "Before Abraham was, I am." He tried to take his hearers back to the sacred name of God in the Old Testament. Regarding that statement, Rabbi Abbahu of Caesarea wrote about 260 A.D.:

> "If a man says, `I am God,' he is a liar, or `I am the son of man,' his end will be such that he will regret it, or `I shall ascend into heaven,' will it not be that he spoke and will not perform it?" [11]

*Writings After the Age of Printing*

Throughout the Middle Ages the New Testament canon remained unchanged as Christianity spread through Western Europe. However, there were some varied interpretations and developments within it.

Both Martin Luther and John Calvin refused submission to the Pope or of the authority of the scriptures to any man or church; but as Christ had said in the New Covenant, the divine authority comes from the inward work of the Holy Spirit within the heart of the believer. Their defense of the independence of the individual believer is a characteristic of the Westminster Confession of Faith published in 1647.[12]

In regard to the criterion of inspiration of the Holy Spirit, <u>H. L. Ellison</u> says, "The writing of the Scriptures was only the half-way house in the process of full understanding and inspiration; it only reaches its goal and conclusion as God is revealed through them to the reader or hearer. In other words, the inbreathing of the Holy Spirit into the reader is as essential for the right understanding of the Scriptures as it was to the original writers for their right production of them."[13]

<u>W. A. Criswell</u>, in his <u>Five Great Questions of the Bible</u>, discusses some of the great geniuses, such as <u>Homer, Virgil, Dante, Shakespeare, and Milton</u>, and says, "Let's put Jesus among them. As gifted as they were, these authors would be amazed to find themselves mentioned in the same breath with Jesus Christ. Shakespeare worked and toiled and saved in order to be financially able to be buried in the chancel of his church. On the stone covering his grave are written these words:

Good friend, for Jesus sake forbeare
To dig the dust enclosed heare.'

In his will Shakespeare wrote, "I commit my soul to God, my creator, in humble belief through the merit of Jesus my Savior to obtain everlasting life."

<u>Charles Lamb</u> and some of his literary associates discussed what they would do if some of the gifted and great of the past were to enter the room. Charles Lamb said, "If Shakespeare were to enter, we would all rise to our feet in admiration, but if Jesus Christ were to enter, we would kneel and worship in adoration."[14]

Through multi-millenniums and the past and present centuries the unanimous belief of man from the first recorded time is the belief that there is some- thing yet beyond the brief experience of life as we know it. The soul and spirit are something other than clay and flesh. Though the philosopher, the cynic, and the metaphysician may scoff and ridicule those who express the belief, Cicero, having made an exhaustive study of the subject concluded, "The immortality of the soul is established by the consent of all peoples."

In the tombs of Egypt when the oldest book ever found was deciphered from the hieroglyphics it was revealed as a book directing the dead to prosperity and happiness in the life beyond the grave.

When the conifer inscriptions on the Chaldean tablets written before Abraham were deciphered, they revealed prayers on behalf of the dead. The inscriptions of ancient Assyrian, Phoenician, Greek, and Roman civilizations all gave testimony to the belief of the life of the soul after death. Such is the subject of <u>Homer's</u> song and of <u>Virgil's</u> Aeneid.[15]

"Without hope of eternal life is like a bridge ending in the midst of a dark abyss." And so it is reinforcing to learn that many of the greatest philosophical minds of history have expressed belief in immortality.

<u>Crito</u>, on the night of <u>Socrates</u> death, asked him, "What way would you like us to bury you?" Socrates replied, "In whatever way that you like. But you must take care that I do not walk away from you."

Plato in his <u>Phaedon</u> gives his powerful argument for his belief in immortality. The same belief is expressed by <u>Thomas Carlyle, Thomas Jefferson, and Heinrich Heine</u>. <u>Goethe</u> expressed it this way, "No matter how strongly we are chained to this earth, a certain intimate longing gives us an inexplicable feeling that we are citizens of another world that shines above us."[16]

<u>Alfred Lord Tennyson</u> wrote:

"For tho' from out our bourne of Time and Place
The flood may bear me far,
I hope to see my Pilot face to face
When I have crossed the bar."

<u>Professor Adolph von Harnack</u> said, "Christ's grave was the birth place of an indestructible belief that death is vanquished and that there is life eternal. The certainty of the resurrection and of a life eternal which is bound up in the grave in Joseph's garden has not perished, and on that knowledge we base our hopes on citizenship in an Eternal City."[17]

Dr. Simon Greenleaf, the Royal Professor of Law at Harvard University referred to in an earlier reference in this document as the greatest authority on legal evidence in the world, turned the searchlight of his immense knowledge upon the resurrection of Jesus Christ and exposed every thread of evidence to the most searching criticism as he sifted the true facts from the false. He came to the conclusion that the evidence was so over- whelming that in any unbiased courtroom in the world that it would be declared to be an absolute historical fact.

Dr. Philip Schaff, an eminent historian and professor at Yale University, wrote in 1865, "From the scores of secular historians and numerous writers of antiquity besides all the evidence we have of the authenticity of the New Testament, standing on this rock of faith, I feel safe against all the attacks of infidelity. The person of Christ is to me the greatest and surest of all facts, as certain as my own existence."

F. F. Bruce, Rylands Professor of Biblical Criticism at the University of Manchester, says, "Some writers may toy with the fancy of a mythical Jesus Christ, but they do not do so on the grounds of historical evidence. The historicity of Christ is as axiomatic as the historicity of Julius Caesar."

He (Bruce) is joined in his opinion by historian J. Gilchrist Lawson who said, "The mythical theory of Christ is not held by anyone worthy of the name of scholar."[18]

Jean Jacques Rousseau, one of the great intellects of France and an opponent of Christianity, later in his life admitted in Emile that there could be no comparison between Socrates and Christ, as little as between a sage and God. Gothe, the sophisticated genius of Germany, said that Jesus was "The Divine Man, the Holy One."[19]

Ernest Renan, the great Oriental scholar, linguist, and critic who tried to tear the Bible to pieces, later called Jesus "a man of colossal dimensions; the incomparable man, to whom the universal conscience has decreed the title of Son of God, and that with justice, since he caused religion to take a greater step than any other in the past and probably any other to come." He closes his Life of Jesus with remarkable concession, "Whatever occurs in the future, Jesus will never be surpassed."

<u>Napoleon Bonapart</u> gave his famous testimony on the island of St. Helena thusly:

> "I know men, and I tell you that Jesus Christ is not just a man. Superficial minds see a resemblance between Christ and the founders of the empires, and the gods of other religions. That resemblance does not exist. There is between Christianity and other religions the distance of infinity. We can say to the authors of religions, `You are not gods nor the agents of the Deity. You are but missionaries of falsehood.' Such will be the judgement, the cry of conscience for whoever examines the gods and temples of paganism. But Jesus Christ astounds me and fills me with awe."[20]

<u>James Greenleaf Whittier</u> said:

> "My ground of hope for myself and for humanity is in that divine fullness of love which was manifested in the life, teaching, and sacrifice of Christ, in the infinite mercy of God so revealed and not in any worth of merit of our nature, I humbly, yet very hopefully trust."

<u>Lord Byron</u> said, "If ever man was God, or God man, Jesus Christ was both."

<u>Charles Dickens</u> said:

> "I commit my soul to the mercy of God, through our Lord and Savior Jesus Christ. I now most humbly impress upon you the truth and beauty of the Christian religion as it came from Christ himself, and the impossibility of going far wrong if you humbly but heartily accept it."[21]

<u>Leo Tolstoy</u>, the great genius of Russian letters who once was an atheist of the wildest order, said this:

"For 35 years of my life I was, in the proper acceptance of the word, a nilist--not a revolutionary socialist, but a man who believed in nothing. Five years ago my faith came to me. I believed in the doctrine of Jesus, and my whole life underwent a sudden transformation. Life and death ceased to be evil; instead of despair, I tasted joy and happiness that death could not take away."[22]

William E. H. Lecky, a great skeptic and unbeliever, author of The History of Rationalism in Europe, analyzed the whole history of thought through all the ages of Europe. He said:

"It was reserved for Christianity to present to the world an Ideal Character, which through all the changes of nineteen centuries, has filled the hearts of men with an impassioned love, and has shown itself capable of acting on all ages, nations, temperaments, conditions, and which has not only been the highest pattern of virtue, but the highest incentive to its practice. Ruskin, Lessing, Webster, Wagner, and innumerable others agree with me."[23]

George Bancroft, the great American historian, says he sees the image of Jesus Christ across every page of modern history.[24]

John Stuart Mill, regarded as one of the most intelligent men who ever lived, called Christ "the guide of humanity."

Frank Morrison, the British lawyer who set out to write a book disproving the resurrection of Christ, did write a book but not the one he intended to write. When he began to examine the evidence, even in his skeptical attitude, he found it so overwhelming that he became a believer and wrote the book, He Moved the Stone, which sets forth the evidence for the resurrection of Christ. He called his first chapter, "The Book That Refused to be Written."

Lew Wallace also planned a book to nullify the deity of Jesus Christ, but ended up writing the famous book Ben Hur. He, along with Royal Professor Simon Greenleaf of Harvard, said, "I have never met one person who has read even one single book on the evidence for the resurrection who did not believe it."[25]

When we review <u>Outline of History</u>, by <u>H. G. Wells</u>, we find his description of the life and death of Jesus Christ. And then he follows with a description of the rise of the Christian church as the largest institution in the history of the world which followed when the disciples began to preach about the resurrection. Any reader plainly sees the connection between the two chapters.

<u>David Strauss</u>, a non-believer, dismissed the swoon theory advanced by other non-believers by saying, "It is impossible that one could come forth from that tomb half dead, needing medical care, could have given an impression that he was a conqueror of death. I don't understand it, but something happened that changed the disciples future ministry. Remember also they subsequently gave their lives in horrible deaths."[26]

<u>Count Zinzendorf</u>, a brilliant, wealthy young German prince, walking through the Duzzeldorf Art Gallery stopped before Ecce Homo, a picture of the suffering Christ. The transcription, "This I have done for thee; what hast thou done for me?," startled him. He left the gallery a changed man who went out to found a powerful missionary endeavor that swept through western Europe.[27]

<u>Lord Shaftsbury</u>, who did more for the social reform of England than perhaps any other person, gave his reason. "I do not think that in the last 40 years I have lived one conscious hour that was not influenced by the thought of our Lord's return. Having this hope, we are sustained and we work to purify ourselves, for justice demands it."[28]

## *Statements Related to Jesus Christ - Gift of the Holy Spirit*

The process of the Holy Spirit entering a life at the time of a person's acceptance of Jesus Christ and His teachings is often referred to as "being born again," because of the whole new focus on life, its meaning, and conduct.

Dr. James Kennedy, the author of <u>Why I Believe the Bible</u>, makes a comparison using the drama of metamorphosis of the caterpillar into the beautiful, productive butterfly which can fly great distances and secures and assists pollination by lighting upon flowers. The poor caterpillar that could hardly jump a millimeter off the ground, yet in the mysterious working of God all things become new--old things pass away and a new creation is formed. As Dr. Kennedy says, "In the same way, God makes a new heart in man."[29]

The belief in the Holy Spirit as a part of the Trinity emerged from the experiences of the first followers of Jesus, who were full-fledged Jews whose affirmation of faith was, "Hear O Israel: the Lord our God, the Lord is One." In Jesus they saw Him do what only God can do--heal folks, quiet the angry sea, and raise people from the dead. He forgave them of their sins and relieved them of their guilt. They couldn't explain Him, but they found themselves worshipping Him. As He prayed to His Father, the God they knew, they were forced to believe in two persons--the Father and the Son. When He talked about leaving them, He assured them that He would send His Holy Spirit to direct them. After Pentecost, they were imbued with that Holy Spirit and finally they realized that the God they had always believed in was able to act in three roles, much as they and we today may be--a father, a son, a husband, a brother, a friend, and perhaps many other roles in our lives, yet we are actually one person.

In A. D. 325 a Church Council of 318 bishops assembled at Nicaea, a little town near the Bosporus Strait. They wrestled with the question of "Who is Jesus Christ?" Together they framed the doctrine of the Trinity. They said He is the true God, of one substance with the Father, thus stating what the earliest followers of Jesus had discovered as they lived with Him. They affirmed that God's love and God's law are one. The God who laid down the law on Mount Sinai also laid down His life on Calvary.[30]

One of the most influential testimonies of the power of the Holy Spirit to completely change a life is when Paul of Tarsus, perhaps Christianity's most rabid antagonist, was stricken blind and Jesus appeared to him. The experience compelled him to acknowledge that Jesus was indeed the Messiah and though he had the most advanced Jewish learning of his day, he was forced to rethink all of his messianic beliefs. Paul went from being an orthodox Pharisee whose mission was to preserve strict Judaism to telling everyone that the Christ who had appeared to him was the Savior of all peoples.[31]

It is not strange that Paul became the most hated of all the Christians of the time because the Jews were taking refuge in their belief that the promised Messiah was yet to come and here one of their own had become a major force against that belief. As Miller Burrows states, "Jesus was so unlike what all Jews expected the son of David to be that Jesus' own disciples found it almost impossible to connect the idea of the Messiah with Him until after His resurrection and Pentecost."[32]

Such testimonies are recorded by numerous well-known persons such as:

William Gladstone, one of England's greatest prime ministers, declared that his life was transformed when he became a believer in Jesus Christ.

Abraham Lincoln tells in his letters that at Gettysburg, the day he gave his famous address, he felt born again, imbued with God's spirit.

Martin Luther, who though a religious man much as Nicodemus to whom Jesus had described the new birth, wrote that he finally felt transformed in his soul.

The writers Fyodor Dostoevski and Leo Tolstoy, of Russia, described how the Holy Spirit transformed their lives.

Chuck Colson after Watergate wrote of his total change in Born Again.

Dr. Benjamin Warfield, a professor of systematic theology at Princeton Theological Seminary, discusses the fact that in the Old Testament the Holy Spirit is not clearly revealed and in the opinion of many theologians is the reason that the Israelites were not able to adhere to God's laws; hence Christ's gift of the Holy Spirit makes a vast difference. Dr. Warfield concludes his analysis thus, "The Old Testament is like a richly furnished but dimly lit room; in the New Testament the light is added."[33]

In John Bunyan's great classic, Pilgrim's Progress, he reminded us that Christian's burden fell off at the cross of Jesus and was seen no more and he went on his way with freedom and joy. The warranty for the promise of eternal life was written in Christ's blood and Christian had received the blessing of the Holy Spirit.[34]

*Jesus' Teachings - Effects on Human Behavior*

James Kennedy discusses the effect of the teachings of Jesus Christ from ancient to modern times on world liberty and freedom for his teachings gave to the individual significant worth. Communism recognizes that the church of Christ is its most formidable foe. He points out that slavery was abolished in England through <u>William Wilberforce</u>, the small hunchbacked man who had become a believer through the preaching of the Wesleys, after which he devoted all of his energy and eloquence to the overthrow of the African slave trade.[35]

A lack of understanding of the basic nature of God has caused many theological and ethical concerns through the years. Many people think of Him only as a loving Father, and He is, but He is also a holy, just, and righteous God.

Adam and Eve, as all human beings, had the opportunity to make their own decisions, and when they rebelled against God and made the decision to sin, at that moment sin entered the human race. Throughout the Bible, we read the phrase, "the wages of sin is death." Propitiation, meaning satisfaction of a requirement was then necessary. So when Jesus died on the cross, He propitiated the payment for human sin but also He met the holy and just requirements of the basic nature of God.

Josh McDowell uses a present day incident to illustrate Jesus' crucifixion in order to solve God's problem in dealing with the sin of humanity:

"A young woman was ticketed for speeding and appeared before a judge. When the judge read off the citation he asked, `Guilty or not guilty?' The young lady replied, `guilty.' The judge brought down the gavel and fined her $100 or ten days in jail. Then an amazing thing took place. The judge stood up, took off his robe, walked down to the police officer's desk, took out his billfold and paid the $100 fine."

"What was the explanation for this? The judge is the father of the young woman who had broken the law. And though he loved her, he was a just judge who must uphold the law. But he loved her so much that he took off his robe as a judge and represented her as her father and paid her fine in propitiation."[36]

Another term borrowed from the court room in relation to man's sin is justification. It defines a declaration that goes beyond "guilty" or "innocent." The old covenant promised physical rewards for physical obedience, but the people did not live up to their part of the agreement. But with the New Covenant there must be a change of heart--an internal change. Justification then is one of the metaphors used to describe salvation. To be justified means that a person is considered to be in the right, and therefore there is no case to judge. But no human being is righteous; therefore, as Paul wrote, "the righteousness of Jesus Christ must be given or imbued to us. If His righteousness is in us, we are justified."[37]

*Statements of Life After Life Experiences*

It has been said that we don't try to prove immortality so that we can believe it; we try to prove it because we can't help believing it.

Other than Jesus' ascension 40 days after His resurrection, we know from the scriptures that "Enoch walked with God and was not" and that "Elijah was taken by a whirlwind into heaven."

It is comforting to believe that life continues after death even if we are not sure about how it happens. "The belief in life after death is strong despite our living in a materialistic, scientific age. In the United States, seven in 10 Americans said in a recent survey that they believe in life after death, and this is generally a steady figure from surveys dating back to the 1940s."[38]

Many scientists have been quite skeptical about the possibility of life beyond the grave. "However, it is worthy of note that recently several scientists have caused quite a stir in the scientific world by announcing that the conclusions of their investigations have led them to believe that life definitely goes on beyond the grave. Their conclusions have been reached from careful, objective interviews with hundreds of persons who had been pronounced dead and later been revived and had told of their experiences during the interval. They report having had a foretaste of either hell or heaven. Since there is no consensus in either medicine or in law as to just when death takes place, these experiences provide interesting, modern testimony to the fact that persons live in either a state of joy or in torment beyond apparent death.[39]

At a national conference at the University of California, Berkeley, on death and dying in the early 90s, Dr. Elizabeth Kubler Ross, a long-time researcher in the field; a psychiatrist, not a Christian, who says that she is not a particularly religious person, shocked a thousand scholars, medical experts, and professional researchers with her opening statement, "The evidence is now conclusive. There is life after death." Her statement came after years of recorded interviews of thousands of medical and psychiatrist researchers all over the world, with children and adults, from all sorts of backgrounds, with a myriad of cultural groups representing the various religions and also agnostic and atheist individuals. Their statements have been carefully analyzed and compiled by objective scientists and the amazing thing has been the unanimity of the testimonials:

- All hear a loud ringing noise and feel themselves moving through a long dark tunnel;
- Each feels that he is outside his body, but able to observe activity of personnel around his body;
- In the majority of cases, the individual becomes aware of an exceedingly bright light, and of an overwhelming presence within that light, universally described as a Christ-like figure, whether or not this individual has ever been exposed to any description of Jesus. This was even true for declared atheists.[40]

- In about one out of seven interviews reported by P. M. H. Atwater who, along with J. S. Levin of the Eastern Virginia Medical School, conducted interviews with over 3,000 near-death individuals, the experience is described as a hell-like experience, and they speak of darkness and terror after they are shown all the events of their life in an indescribable panorama.[41]
- The individual glimpses and recognizes spirits of deceased relatives and friends. Many recall seeing other realms of existence that are described in terms "remarkably like biblical descriptions of heaven, even by persons who know little of the Bible."[42]

Dr. Norman Vincent Peale reported a story shared with him by a physician who said, "Dr. Peale, a startling thing happened to me. I was at the bedside of a dying patient who opened his eyes and looked up smiling. Then he called out to his mother and father and his brother and sister. Then he said, `Frank, I didn't know you were there.' Then he died. Along with me at the bedside was his daughter who said, `That's odd; my grand-parents, uncle, and aunt died years ago, but Dad's cousin, Frank, is still alive.' When she returned home, a telegram was waiting for her announcing that Frank had died in an accident just a few hours before."[43]

- Finally the person reports that he was told to return to the living. If he has had the experience of light, love, and peace as described in the best-selling book, Embraced by the Light, by Betty J. Eadie, he begs to be allowed to stay in this beautiful place. But for those who had a frightening experience, they are pleased to return. But according to Dr. Moody's books, Life After Life and Reflections on Life After Life, these persons' lives were changed after their near-death experience.[44]

Kennedy, in his book Why I Believe, says "that in the quotes of last words, we know how people face death. We find in the words of Edward Gibbon, a noted infidel, `All is dark.' But in the last words of Augustus Toplady, author of the hymn, Rock of Ages, `all is light, light, light!' Dr. Kennedy reminds us that the Bible makes it "abundantly clear that there is a heaven, but also that everyone is not going there. The question is <u>not</u> whether, but simply <u>where</u> we will spend eternity."[45]

In the foreword of Betty J. Eadie's New York Times best seller book, <u>Embraced by the Light</u>, Melvin Morse, M. D., states:

> "Near-death experiences are not caused by a lack of oxygen to the brain, or drugs, or psychological stresses evoked by the fear of dying. Almost 20 years of scientific research has documented an area in the brain which allows us to have these experiences as a natural, normal process. That means that near-death experiences are absolutely real and are not hallucinations of the mind. Betty Eadie learned by nearly dying what the great prophets and spiritual leaders have tried to tell us for thousands of years."[46]

<u>Dr. Kubler Ross</u> said in conclusion to her colleagues at the Berkeley conference, "We now have factual support, replicated again and again, in thousands of cases by different people from all over the world. For me, there is no longer a shadow of a doubt. I used to say, `I believe in life after death.' Now I <u>know</u>." The 1,000 medical professionals, scholars, and researchers in that audience stood to give this psychiatrist a standing ovation.[47]

*Recent Statements About Jesus*

<u>C. S. Lewis</u>, the Oxford professor who says that he went "kicking and screaming" in the process of accepting Christianity over atheism, says, "People often say of Christ, I'm ready to accept Jesus as a great moral teacher, but I don't accept Him as the Son of God. That's the one thing we mustn't say. A man who was merely a man and said the sort of things Jesus said wouldn't be a great moral teacher. He'd be either a lunatic or the devil. You must make your choice. Either this man was, and is, the Son of God, or else a mad man or something worse. You can shut Him up as a

fool, you can spit on Him, kill Him as a demon, or you can fall at His feet and worship Him. But don't come with any patronizing nonsense about His being a great moral teacher. He has not left that open to us. He didn't intend to."

"He gives us the chance to join Him freely. I don't suppose you and I would think much of a Frenchman who waited until the Allies were marching into Berlin and then announced that he was on their side. I wonder if people realize what it will be like when He comes. It will be the end of the world and too late then to choose. That day is unavoidable and the consequences of that day are irreversible. We know when the author walks onto the stage the play is over. Now is our chance to decide. It won't last forever; we must take it or leave it. We must realize that the central belief of Christianity is none other than this: Christ's death has somehow put us right with God and thus has given us a fresh start."[48]

Josh McDowell, whose writings I have used to illuminate points in this manuscript and who was one of the driving forces in the development of the American organization of Christian Athletes had a similar struggle with accepting Christianity as did C. S. Lewis.

As a university professor, he began to notice a group of persons who were different. They seemed to know what they believed and why they believed. They appeared to possess an inner source of joy and he stated they were "disgustingly happy." He finally broke down and asked them what made them so different. They had one answer, "Jesus Christ."

McDowell's response was, "Oh, for God's sake, don't give me that garbage. I'm fed up with religion." "One of the young ladies shot back the response, 'Sir, I didn't say religion. I said Jesus Christ.' She quietly pointed out something I had never thought about before--that religion is humans trying to work their way to God through good works. Christianity is God coming to men and women through Jesus, offering them a relationship with himself."

McDowell goes on to say that there are probably more people in our universities with misconceptions about Christianity than anywhere else.

McDowell's first two books were setting out to refute Christianity. He says, "When I couldn't, I ended up becoming a believer and since then I have spent years documenting why I believe that faith in Jesus is intellectually feasible. I'm sure you have heard religious persons talking about the bolt of lightning they felt when they became a believer, I guess something like Paul experienced. Well, I felt nothing. I wondered if I had gone off the deep end. But in about six months, I was aware that my life had changed. I no longer thought Christians were walking idiots. I no longer waited for a Christian to speak up in class so I could tear his ideas to bits. I felt the love that Jesus promised to enter my life and take the hatred and turn it upside down. I could even say to my father who had been the town alcoholic through my growing up that I forgave him and that I loved him. In time, my dad also became a believer and was changed right before my eyes. Jesus has never given up the business of changing lives. But Christianity is not something to be forced on anyone, like the Spanish Inquisition, or in modern times by over zealous denominations. We each have our own decisions to make and our lives to live, but we each need to research and learn about God's offer through His Son. What I try to do is to share what I have learned. After that, it is each individual's decision."[49]

*Celebrated Athletes' Statements*

Dave Dravecky, the pitcher for the San Francisco Giants, who kept coming back after the removal of numerous cancerous tumors from his pitching arm finally had to accept the medical fact that he must retire. The sports world grieved for him, but he accepted that final shoulder break during the game with Montreal and stated, "I wasn't as thankful for the miracle of coming back as for the larger miracle of the gift of salvation God has given me through Jesus. I am at peace and believe that God is calling me in a new direction."[50]

Danny Wuerffel, the 1996 Heisman Trophy winner in football, is a member of the Fellowship of Christian Athletes and has given leadership to many campus projects at the University of Florida. He spoke at the trophy ceremony giving credit for his athletic success to his following the teachings of Jesus.[51]

Dr. Louis Goldberg, Professor of Theology and Jewish Studies at the Moody Bible Institute in Chicago, writes that as an engineer a colleague insisted that he read the Bible. He said at that time he could accept the Hebrew Scriptures as a part of his heritage, but that his university years had led him to be an agnostic. He says that he knew a lot about his Jewish background, the holidays, and how to read the Torah in the synagogue. So to help get rid of his agnosticism, he began to read to find answers. He said, "If I had trouble accepting the Old Testament as authoritative, what was I to do with Jesus and the New Testament?" What startled me was the fact that all of the writers of the New Testament, with the exception of Luke, were Jewish. They wrote with great knowledge of Jewish history, background, and culture. As I compared the prophesies from the Old Testament with the documented activities of Jesus's life, I saw that he was the fulfillment of all of the early prophets. And I thought that if a so-called Messiah appears now, how will his lineage be properly traced since the Jerusalem temple containing all of the genealogy data was destroyed in 70 A.D. So could I accept the New Testament Canon along side that of the Old Testament? There was no other choice but to do so, when confronted with the internal, external bibliographic, historical, and prophetic evidence of Jesus's life and influence on the world for over two millennia."[52]

## *Pilate Attributes Rescue to Faith*

Recently during the United Nations' attempts to bring some semblance of understanding among the factions in Bosnia, the narrow escape of American F-16 Pilot, Scott O'Grady, who had been shot down in open country in Bosnia made international news. He attributed his astounding ability to evade the Serbs, who were often within feet of him, to the belief that Jesus Christ's ability to project the weak sound of his beeper to the planes overhead, who were seeking him for days, so that he would be saved. However, he reported when finally rescued that if the final result had been different that his prayer had been that he would be faithful to his faith under any circumstances.

## Chinese Communist Becomes A Christian

Very recently, <u>Hong Yang</u>, a rising star in China's Communist Party, after serrupticiously reading a banned Bible he had stumbled upon was willing to surrender all--his country, his career, and his wife--to come to the United States to study theology. He was an atheist who had denounced Christianity as a "superstition of the blue-eyed devils." As Yang studied the Bible secretly, he had a series of visions or dreams for seven nights in which a blooded figure would say to him, "By my brokenness, you will be made whole." He says that he had read the works of Aristotle, Emerson, and Kierkegard, but they never satisfied him. He said, "I was particularly moved by the courage, the suffering, and the honesty of Jesus. And I knew that it was He who was speaking to me." So through two American English teachers whom he met, he was able to arrange to come to Tennessee to study because the Communist Party thought he was coming to study technology, not theology. Though his wife had denounced his conversion to Christianity, she has now followed him to Tennessee. He says today, "I made the right decision--the one the rich young ruler of Jesus's parable did not make."[53]

## The Jesus Seminar

As the 2000th anniversary of the birth of Jesus nears, an intellectual tug of war continues about who Jesus was, what he said and did as the era of skepticism and biblical illiteracy continues. The media savvy Jesus Seminar, a nationally known conclave of liberal Bible scholars "chips away at the centuries-old image of Jesus in their annual meetings." "Fellows of the Jesus Seminar, organized in 1985 by former Emory University professor, <u>Robert Funk</u>, casts their votes by colored marbles signifying probability--a black ball means the voter believes that something <u>did not happen</u>; gray means <u>probably did not</u> happen; pink means <u>probably did</u>; and red means the scholar is certain that an event or saying <u>did</u> occur. However, for the first time the Seminar is inviting ordinary people in who are on the cutting edge of the debate, according to Catholic scholar <u>John Dominac Crossan</u>, co-chair."

"Now after years of ignoring the Seminar, or berating the orthodox way it sifts history, scholars on the more traditional side are responding with books, conferences, and lecture tours, arguing that good scholarship does not have to separate the Jesus Christ of faith from the Jesus Christ of history. The impact of the Jesus Seminar and its left-wing scholars has been so pervasive that it has to be reckoned with," said Gregory Boyd of Bethel College in St. Paul, Minnesota.[54]

Some of the statements of the members of the Seminar reveal the professorial disagreements that typify the Seminar sessions:

<u>George Vanderlin</u> of Fuller Theological Seminary, Pasadena, California, says, "Liberalism can be intense on both sides. One side is obsessed with the accuracy of every word and letter of the scripture, while the other side is equally focused on scientific and historical truths. Unfortunately, when we get hung up on arguing about symbols, we miss the truth behind them. That's the tragedy of it!"

<u>Marcus Borgs</u>', professor of Religion and Culture at Oregon State University, own spiritual journey is discussed in his book, <u>Meeting Jesus Again for the First Time</u>, where he says, "I knew that Jesus was born of a virgin before I even knew what a virgin was. But with increasing skepticism, I went from being a young literalist to an adult atheist before coming back into the faith as a non-literalist."

<u>Moessner</u> of Columbia Theological Seminary says, "What Jesus stood for in his lifetime and the resurrected living Christ in the world today are what count. It is not incredible to believe that the God who created the universe and raised Jesus from the dead could certainly make a virgin pregnant."

<u>John P. Meier</u>, a Catholic priest and professor of New Testament at Catholic University in Washington said, "The important issue is the relationship between the historical

accounts and the message of faith they are intended to convey. Christianity, unlike some religions, is connected to a historical event--the life of Jesus."

Luke Johnson, professor of New Testament at Emory University's Candler School of Theology says, "The only thing the professors have given is the ability to dissect the text into 'itty-bitty' pieces, so it is like going to medical school and being taught only how to perform autopsies."[55]

A number of critics say that as extreme as the members of the Jesus Seminar are, as they discard much of the gospels as fabrications, they do believe that in the "simple, moving, and transcendently beautiful messages of the parables that we come as close to the historical Jesus as we are likely to get. His parables contain striking images, dramatic action, and bold character development, all built around universal themes that have touched and changed lives for two millennia."[56]

*Other Scholars' Views*

A broad spectrum of international scholars see no real reason to reject the Gospels. Research has brought new insights from the Jewish studies and their archeological findings.

"Advocates range from hardline fundamentalists and moderate evangelicals, who all along have deemed the Gospels historically trustworthy, to moderate liberals who use high criticism, but recently have become skeptical about their own skepticism."

Peter Stuhlmacher of Tubingen University in Germany has said, "As a Western Scripture scholar I am inclined to doubt these Gospel stories, but as a historian, I am obliged to judge them to be reliable. The biblical texts as they stand are the best hypothesis we have to explain what happened." Scholars like Stuhlmacher make no excuses and seek no secularized explanations for the miracles of the New Testament.

The sophisticated historian, F. F. Bruce, whose work has been cited earlier in this document said, "The historian has to take into account that Jesus's opponents conceded that He did perform miracles. If Jesus is God's Son as He claimed to be, then miracles are what one would expect."

It has been admitted by many scholars that they had never visited the Holy Land and that they had totally neglected the influence of Jewish culture on Jesus--"a bad tradition with limited results" according to Martin Hengel of Tubingen University. So the turning away from skepticism toward a renewed acceptance of Jesus and His teachings comes from the new evidence learned from the recent studies of Jewish culture in first century Palestine.

An international panel of 34 evangelical scholars in their 1987 report, The Historical Reliability of the Gospels, stated, "It is fair to say that all the alleged inconsistencies among the Gospels have received at least plausible resolutions."[57]

*Current Secular Statements About Jesus*

As Norman Mailer refers to his new first person novel, The Gospel According to the Son, he says, "My intent is neither pious nor satirical; it is instead to make comprehensible for myself what Fulton Oursler once called 'The Greatest Story Ever Told.'"[58]

Amy Vershup in the George Magazine anniversary issue reports the testimony of Jay Schulow, a marriage lawyer from Mercer University Law School, who said: "What attracted me to faith was Jesus himself. Not Christianity as a religion, but Jesus as a relationship--what He did, what He stood for. When I acknowledged Jesus as the Messiah that began my journey. There were a lot of bumps in the road for me. Conversion is a process. We are always in a process of converting to something, whether it is a belief or a world view. I believe there is actually no conflict between believing that Jesus is the Messiah and being Jewish for he fulfills the prophesies that we Jews already believe. When we search for truth, we don't get there in a few minutes. I asked God for a second chance, and He gave it to me, and I became a believer. The Christians have something to say to us, and we need to listen." President Jimmy Carter discusses the innate desire of Everyman for a personal relationship with God in his recent book, Living Faith. He reminds us that desire cannot be abolished even under the greatest pressure, as evidenced by the disintegration of the once powerful Soviet Union. Karl Marx had said, "Religion is the opium of the people," 80 years after religion was replaced with atheism the seed of faith still existed and "there is now an explosion of religious fervor in Russia."

President Carter speaks of his own faith, "In my early life, the varied, even paradoxical qualities of Jesus were obstacles to my faith. Only over the years and through the powerful examples of peoples' lives have I begun to realize what they really mean. I have come to realize that the apparent weaknesses of Jesus gave Him a quality of authenticity that I find are what makes Him convincing. Perhaps the most exalting statement He ever made was to His disciples in their last meeting in which He emphasized His status as the Messiah; after which He undressed, wrapped in a towel, knelt on the floor, and washed their feet. To me personally, Jesus bridges the tremendous chasm between human beings and the seemingly remote and omnipotent God the Creator. It really comforts and satisfies me to equate the Almighty Creator with the humble Jesus. He helps me to remember that `God is love.'"[59]

In 1988, in Washington, D. C., at a joint conference of educators and inventors, Dr. Raymond Demadian was my dinner partner at a banquet. In conversation, I found him unbelievably modest about his success in inventing the MRI, the magnetic resonance scanner, which is used to detect all diseases, but its greatest use is in searching for cancer, thus saving thousands of lives. After reading his story in Decision, I better understood his modesty. He gives credit for his success as an inventor to the guiding of the Holy Spirit. He describes his experience this way, "There is a mistaken impression that science and God are not compatible. As a scientist and a Christian, I believe that to be wrong. Science ought to unite men and women to their Creator rather than separate them from Him."

"It was during my first year in medical school that I discovered that it is possible to have a personal relationship with God through Jesus Christ. Donna Terry, who later became my wife, invited me to the Billy Graham Crusade in Madison Square Gardens. That night I was convinced of the Lordship of Jesus Christ, and I went forward at Dr. Graham's invitation and gave my life to Him."

"When I began my professional career as a professor of biophysics at the New York Medical Center, I recognized that God is the source of creativity and scientific insight and is responsible, I believe, for the contributions I have made to the present-day understanding of cell theory and ultimately to the invention of the MRI. For from the outset, I was told that making a machine like this could not be done. Funding agencies considered the project nonsense and thought I was a fool. But I didn't give up trying. I am certain that I can contribute my willingness to go ahead to my ability to trust it to the Lord. The Holy Spirit was working in me to get the job done."

"My faith has been the foundation of my life, and I am grateful that my position as the CEO of Fonar Corporation gives me the opportunity to share the Gospel message in scientific circles."[60]

*Everyman's Responsibility*

As these statements of belief by persons recorded through the ages reveal, Everyman has need of a stable strength beyond himself, and we are individually responsible to keep searching until we find that true source of power.

For persons exploring the nature of God and His relationship with man, the holocaust presents one of the greatest challenges of all time. Auschwitz confronts the whole world with guilt, and as more and more information is revealed in recent days, our inescapable need for atonement is illuminated, according to Ulrich Simon, who escaped Germany during the holocaust to become a priest in England. In his A Theory of Auschwitz--The Christian Faith and The Problem of Evil, he makes Everyman aware of his need for healing and a reconciliation with God on His terms, and not ours.

Everyman knows that he is responsible for the propaganda that he believes  and for his failure to explore every opportunity to discern truth and thereby to make decisions. Shirley Guthrie, professor of systematic theology at Columbia Theological Seminary says, "God does not make robots. God makes persons who make choices. He knows that also means the possibility of <u>Everyman</u> making wrong decisions; but, nevertheless, He allows us that freedom."[61]

# REFERENCES FOR SECTION III

1. Kennedy, Dr. James. Why I Believe the Bible. Word Books, Publisher, Waco, Texas, 1981, pp. 96-98.

2. Greene, Michael. Who Is This Jesus. Thomas Nelson Publishers, Nashville, Tennessee, 1992, pp. 116-118.

3. Ibid, pp. 24-25.

4. Ibid, p. 116.

5. Ibid, p. 117.

6. Ibid, p. 114.

7. Ibid, p. 46.

8. Kennedy, Why I Believe, pp. 99 and 120.

9. Schaff, Phillip. Testimonies of Unbelievers, American Tract Society, Boston, 1865, p. 281.

10. Bowie, Walter Russell. Men of Fire. Harper Brothers Publishing, New York, 1961, Chapter 6.

11. Greene, p. 60.

12. Bruce, F. F. The Canon of Scripture. Intervarsity Press, Downer's Grove, Illinois, 1988, p. 249.

13. Ibid, p. 282.

14. Criswell, W. A. Five Great Questions of the Bible. Zondervan Publishing House, Grand Rapids, Michigan, 1958, p. 35.

15. Ibid, pp. 21-22.
16. Kennedy, Why I Believe. p. 64.

17. Peters, Madison C. After Death What? Christian Herald, New York, 1908, pp. 166-167.

18. Greenleaf, Dr. Simon. An Examination of the Testimony of the Four Evangelists by the Rules of Evidence Administered in the Courts of Justice. Baker Book House, Grand Rapids, Michigan, 1965. (Reprint of 1874 edition, New York, Cockroft and Company, 1874.)

19. Kennedy, Why I Believe, p. 100.

20. Ibid, pp. 101-102.

21. Lawson, J. Gilchrist. Greatest Thoughts About Jesus Christ.

Richard R. Smith Company, New York, 1919, pp. 117-120.

22. Ibid, p. 121.

23. Kennedy, Why I Believe, p. 102.

24. Ibid, pp. 106-107.

25. Ibid, p. 108.

26. Ibid, pp. 108 and 116.

27. Criswell, p. 54.

28. Kennedy, Why I Believe, p. 152.

29. Ibid, pp. 135-136.

30. Decision Magazine.  Billy Graham Association, Minneapolis, Minnesota, May 1993, "The Mystery of the Trinity," pp. 16-17.

31. McDowell, Josh.  More Than A Carpenter, Living Book Series, Lyndale Publishing, Wheaton, Illinois, 1973, pp. 81-84.

32. Ibid, p. 74.

33. Ibid, p. 142.

34. Greene, op. cit., p. 74.

35. Kennedy, Why I Believe, p. 124.

36. McDowell, op. cit., pp. 114-115.

37. The Plain Truth Magazine.  The Plain Truth Ministry, Pasadena, California, October, 1992, p. 8.

38. Ibid, May 1992, p. 18.

39. Moody, Raymond.  "Life After Life," a brochure by Guidepost, Carmel, New York.

40. Kennedy, James.  Evangelism Explosion, Tyndale House Publishing, Wheaton, Illinois, 1983, pp. 102-103.

41. Miller, Leslie.  "Can Science Lift a Shroud of Mystery?" News article in U.S.A. Today, June 1996.

42. Moody, "Life After Life" brochure by Guidepost.

43. Shuler, Dr. Robert.  "At Last Proof of Eternal Life!"  Hour of Power Publishing, Garden Grove, California, 1973.

44.    Moody, "Life After Life" brochure by Guidepost.

45. Kennedy, Why I Believe, p. 68.

46. Eadie, Betty J. Embraced by the Light, Bantam Books, 1994, Foreword.

47. Kennedy, Evangelism Explosion, p. 102.

48. Lewis, C. S. The Case for Christianity, Macmillan Publishing Company, New York, 1989, pp. 45, 46, 56.

49. McDowell, Josh. "He Changed my Life," from newspaper, North Peachtree Messenger, Atlanta, Georgia, April 1993, pp. 8-9.

50. Dravecky, Dave. "Stepping off the Mound," Decision Magazine, Billy Graham Association, Minneapolis, Minnesota, March 1990, pp. 4-5.

51. "Power Christianity," Atlanta Constitution, December 14, 1996, p. G4.

52. Goldberg, Louis. "What About this Book," Decision Magazine, Billy Graham Association, Minneapolis, Minnesota, February 1995, pp. 12-13.

53. "An Ex-Atheist Leaves China--Surrendering All as a Christian," Atlanta Constitution, March 8, 1997, p. F4.

54. "Historic Jesus at Center of Scholarly Tug of War," Atlanta Journal- Constitution, October 29, 1995, p. H10.

55. "Jesus: Scholars Ponder Miracle of Birth," Atlanta Journal-Constitution, December 25, 1994, p. H5.

56. Shoaf, Norman L. "What Jesus's Parables Reveal," The Plain Truth Magazine, July 1993, p. 6.

57. Time Magazine, August 15, 1988, pp. 38-41.

58. Mailer, Norman. The Gospel According to the Son, Random House, New York, 1997.

59. Carter, President Jimmy. Living Faith, Times Book by Random House, New York, 1996, pp. 33 and 233.

60. "The Story of Dr. Raymond Demadian," Decision Magazine, September 1992, p. 23.

61. "Evil: Beyond Human Power," Atlanta Journal-Constitution, May 7, 1995, p. B2.

# SECTION IV

# THE SEARCH FOR TRUTH

*Truth As A Priority*

Throughout our lives, at our early idealistic stage, and particularly at the mature adult stage, we perceive a stirring need to pursue truth, progressively and often passionately. Early on, we question much that is handed down to us by our families, our religions, our educators, and our various societies. We find that there are numerous answers, varied opinions, and much low-level reasoning. Finally, in time, we come to realize that the significance of our pursuit of truth lies in coming up with the right questions.

Searching diligently for answers to the right questions then clears the haze around many of life's delusions, opens our minds and hearts to Everyman's needs and gives us a constant enthusiasm for the pursuit of the most meaningful truths that mankind has faced through the ages.

We begin to see examples in life of the authority of truth, such as is evidenced by Mother Theresa who defined by her life the distinction between power and authority. Though she had no power based on strength, she had incredible authority. There were no lines drawn in the sand, nor were there arguments or disagreements; she simply did what God had called her to do with no concern for the personal costs. "We know that authority is deeply rooted in the truth, and the humble acting out of that truth in loving ways." Mother Theresa learned a truth from the Jesus she followed for her 86 years which she passed on to us, "If you take time to judge people, you have no time to love and serve them."[1]

Jacob Bronowski discussed the two ways of looking for truth in his book Science and Human Values: He says, "One way is to find concepts that are beyond challenge because they are held by faith, or authority, or the conviction that they are self-evident."

St. Thomas Aquinas held that faith is a higher guide to truth than knowledge. Peter Abelard challenged that notion and said, "All truth, even the highest type, is accessible to test. By doubting, we are led to inquire, and by inquiring we perceive actual truth."[2]

Victor Frankel, the Viennese psychiatrist who survived Auchwitz, reminds us that "if we let our search for truth become too specialized, we may no longer see the forest of truth if we dwell only on the trees of facts."[3]

Elie Wiesal, Nobel Laureate, speaks of the faith of Maria, the simple, uneducated Christian maid who gave his family a choice during the days of the Third Reich to surreptitiously follow her to a secluded mountain cabin to insure their safety. But they chose to believe the false promises of the Nazi authorities instead, and his parents and a sister died in a concentration camp. He speaks of his admiration for Maria's strength of faith as the only person, in a town of intellectuals, dignitaries, and clergy, who showed strength of character and true living faith. He refers particularly to the elite who never raised their voices by saying, "Of what value was their education, social position, and their so-called faith when they showed neither conscience nor compassion."[4]

"There is also the answer of indifference to truth, which Pilate gave to the question he himself asked, `What is truth?' and `What do I do with Jesus?' He is a perfect example of that vain, shallow indifference, which is too weak to believe in truth and yet too fearful to deny it altogether."[5]

As I pursued the truth to find realistic answers to the four questions I posed years ago, I often found myself in the posture of Paul de Kruif, former editor of <u>Reader's Digest</u>, who said that one of his greatest shortcomings in his spiritual life was, "My worship of my own reasoning." When we have been a believer for many years, we tend to repeat those "pat" answers that we have heard so many times in sermons and accept them without further thought. However, as we sincerely pursue comprehensive answers, we grow in grace in our faith, combined with an intellectual stimulation, for when we find reasonable specific answers which satisfy our spiritual curiosity, we are humbled and experience a fair-minded balance of thought which surprises even ourselves.

*Spirituality Versus Religion*

As we focus on the spiritual, we realize that spirituality implies something highly personal and transcendent, whereas religion deals more with the material side of life--with the secular. "Our psyche seeks a religious image, an experience by which to express the mysteries of the spirit."[6] Because we are spiritual creatures we yearn to rise above the linearity of time so that we can connect with the eternal, and we seek to understand more about eternity. As believers we expect to move into eternity as life ceases, and we seek to understand what it involves.

William Munsey discusses the characteristics of the scant knowledge we have of eternity, and he finally states, "Eternity is an infinite circle that cannot be measured or explained." Both Munsey and Jimmy Carter say that it is an aspect that our earthly minds cannot fully comprehend. But they remind us, Jesus never said that we are to understand. He said, "Only believe."[7]

As intelligent, independent thinkers we often find the business of living has a way of crowding spirituality out and creating the dangerous illusion that we alone are the masters of our own fate. But when Everyman prayerfully seeks and finds answers to his spiritual questions and reaches the decision-making level, he realizes that indeed his decisions about the significance of Jesus's death, the New Covenant opportunity, and the veracity of their proof in the New Testament does determine his destiny as it relates to eternity.

*Relationship of Faith and Works*

As Everyman follows up with a decision to accept the veritable truths, he then must decide on a plan of action. "It is said that our American work ethic leads us to a bias toward a works reward. People assume that salvation and heaven are a reward, because they know that they must earn such things as their paycheck, their home, their car, and their retirement annuity. The difference is that salvation, which comes to Everyman as he believes in Jesus, is not a payoff but the establishment of a relationship with Him. Relationships can never be earned. They are always given and received. If that is true at the human level, how much more so is our relationship at the spiritual level."[8]

Jesus taught the good news that the kingdom comes to each of us as a gift once we believe. He expects believers to live according to God's will, but that is altogether different than thinking that a rigid set of rules and laws can earn salvation. His advice was to ask for divine guidance in using one's individual initiative: "Ask and it shall be given to you; seek and you will find; knock and the door will be opened to you."

The person who seeks to gain salvation as a reward for his good behavior is placing his faith wholly in himself. The person who seeks to gain heaven by God's grace is placing his faith in Jesus's promise and accepting what He has already done for man.[9]

Perhaps the story of the old Scotsman who operated a small rowboat for transporting tourists across a small lake in the Scotch Highlands will give Everyman a realistic perspective:

"One day a passenger noticed that the Scotsman had carved on one oar `WORKS' and on the other oar the word `FAITH'. Curiosity led him to ask the meaning of this. The old man replied, `I'll show you.' So dropping the oar called FAITH and plying with the one called WORKS only, of course, they just went around in circles. Then he dropped the WORKS oar and began to ply the one labeled FAITH and the little boat went around in circles again--this time in the opposite direction."

"After the demonstration, the old man picked up both the FAITH and the WORKS oars and plying both oars together sped swiftly over the water, explaining to his inquiring passenger, `You see, that is the way it is in life. Without faith, life would be empty, but then faith without works would be useless."[10]

*Intelligent Faith Gives Freedom*

Everyman will find as he studies the Scriptures that when a person is called upon to exercise faith, it is an intelligent faith that is required. Jesus emphasized over and over, "You shall know the truth, and the truth will set you free." When He was asked, "What is the greatest commandment of all?", His answer was, "To love the

78

Lord with all your heart and with all your <u>mind</u>." We find many believers who seem to stop with their hearts who never take the time and study that is necessary to allow Jesus to get to their minds. The Holy Spirit innovates our minds with the desire to know God as well as the heart to love Him. We need to function fully in both areas to have the maximum relationship that He desires for us. "He does not want endless, mindless servants. He, as our loving heavenly Father, wants instead sons and daughters who intellectually believe and who follow through with the Eleventh Commandment which Jesus added to the Ten--`Love thy neighbor as thyself.'"[11]

In recent years we have realized the tragedy of mind control tactics, as great nations with centuries of historic achievement, such as China, Russia, and Germany have fallen prey to controlling leaders of Communism and Nazism and the populace became zombie-like followers. We have seen it in segmented groups like the mindless followers of Jim Jones, David Karesh, and Marshall Applewhite, who isolated followers from reality and instead of seeking truth in an open, realist environment let themselves be brain-washed by demented extremists who assumed the role of a savior.

As Jesus told Annas in the first stages of His trial that He had always spoken openly in the synagogue and elsewhere to persons who come of their own volition and who decided on their own whether or not they wanted to become followers, "true divinity always awaits the expression of man's free will, as determined by his own intellectual decision. Jesus and the spiritual hierarchy never--no matter the need nor important the incentive--infringe on the divine right of man to make his own decisions and to exercise his own free will."[12] The Spanish Inquisition and such unfortunate incidents of history were only politically, not spiritually, motivated.

Yes, <u>Everyman</u> indeed has the choice to make mistakes in judgment and hence suffer serious and often sadly detrimental consequences.

Many Christian denominations believe in the priesthood of the believer; that is, each believer can communicate directly with God and is not dependent on an intercessor, such as a minister, priest, or rabbi. As a consequence, each individual is responsible to seek truth, intellectually and spiritually, through study and prayer for the cultivation of his inner life, as well as a responsibility for the development of a sincere concern for the welfare of his fellowman.

## Technological Spiritual Outreach

For over two thousand years there has been recorded speculation as to the end of time as we know it. As Jesus entreated His followers to take the gospel to all corners of the earth, He said, "And this gospel of the kingdom shall be preached in all the world for a witness to all nations, and then shall the end come."

For the first time in history, the gospel is being spread rapidly, through recent technology, to even the most remote areas of the world. In 1995 and 1996, the Global Mission (established by the Billy Graham Association) positioned powerful satellites in locations above Puerto Rico, Europe, the Middle East, and the Far East, allowing transmission of the gospel message across all continents simultaneously. Two hundred countries reported preparedness and eagerness for the broadcast, from the smallest villages to the largest cities. Hundreds of millions saw the program by satellite, while cable operators in scores of countries took the message off the satellite broadcast and beamed it into millions of additional homes. A total of 500,000 pastors and between 800,000 and 1 million Christian workers prayerfully prepared their communities to receive the message. Three hundred interpreters in 45 languages were strategically placed in regions around the world to interpret the message into additional languages and dialects. A half billion pieces of literature to support the message were translated and distributed through local venues worldwide as a support for preparation and follow-up of viewers.

In 1981, it was reported that 1,320,000,000 persons worldwide claimed to be believers in Jesus Christ. The summary reports from Global Mission broadcasts in 1995 indicated one billion viewers, and the 1996 report indicated at least 2.5 billion persons viewed the telecast. Viewers of both telecasts are receiving support follow-up broadcasts, films, videos, literature, and personal contacts presently.[13]

The projected estimate of 70 percent of the world's population of 5.4 billion to receive the Global Mission broadcast encouraged the financial support and prayers of millions of Christians to make these far-reaching endeavors possible.

*Present World Conditions*

In spite of all the scientific and technological advances, human nature has changed very little since the days of Adam. As the world has shrunk in time and space, we are made more and more aware of the violence, hatred, lust, starvation, greed, cruelty, indifference, and corruption that exists at family, societal, and international levels. And at the same time, the reverberations of the human heart for love and forgiveness, for real meaning, for hope, and for peace remind us that those are the issues Jesus spent His time on earth addressing. We must remember that He never said that we would be excused from life's trials. He certainly wasn't. However, He promised His peace would always be with believers, giving them strength to endure, as they returned good for evil, and showed love instead of hate.

Michael Horowitz, a member of the Hudson Institute staff, is full of consternation for the world leaders who ignore the present-day religious persecution of Christian remnant populations in the Soviet Union, Pakistan, Iran, Ethiopia, Turkey, China, and the Sudan. It is said that more persecution of religious faiths has occurred in this century than in all the centuries before. Horowitz chastises the United Nations and heads of state who swore, following the Holocaust that destroyed millions of his people, that such inhumane treatment would never again be tolerated. Yet today, thousands are starved in refugee camps, gas bombed, or sprayed with hot oil as they attempt to escape. He reports that 30,000 child slaves are reported in the Sudan, while monetary rewards and political favors are given to citizens who report the existence of Bible study groups in most of the aforementioned countries.[14]

Though according to our current news reports and Horowitz's expressed concerns about the evil which continues to abort justice and decency in human behavior, there are recent reports of some Christian groups around the world who are seeking forgiveness for historical transgressions.

The Pope asked Catholics to repent to hundreds of German Christians and Jews for the atrocities of the Nazi era. Southern Baptists, the largest U. S. Protestant body, formally apologized to blacks for endorsing slavery over a century ago after their 1995 convention.

French Protestants and Catholics said prayers of remorse for the thousands of Moslems that the European Knights slew in the name of Jesus during the Medieval Crusades. Lutherans have asked forgiveness for the Anti-Semitism of their founder, Martin Luther. New Zealanders have confessed their sins against the Maoris. American Christians have prayed on Indian reservations for forgiveness for the white man's massacre of Native Americans. Japanese Christians have been bolder than their waffling government and have asked forgiveness for Pearl Harbor.[15]

As Everyman reviews what has occurred internationally in the last two decades, he sees some surprising peace movements.

Russia, after nearly 70 years of atheism and political isolation opened up to Christian Orthodoxy which all that time had survived underground. It is estimated that there are 60 million believers in the former Communist East European countries. The leader of Russia's Communist Party has put down Marx and Lenin and is now relying on the Bible and Russia's war heroes as the inspiration for his new political endeavors. One questions his approach to the proletariat by paralleling the comeback of a so-called different Communist Party to Jesus's attempt to bring justice by sacrificing His life to atone for other people's sins. We trust that the Russian intelligencia, many of whom have serrupticiously remained Christian, will discern Zyuganov's ploy.[16]

The timing of the fall of the Berlin Wall surprised not only the Western world, but the whole world, as well. It is reported now that prayer meetings inside, as well as outside, East Germany supported the peaceful revolution. Particularly involved over a long period of time were the Christians in the Leipzig area.

Poland's solidarity continues as a non-violent Christian rebellion.

North Korea, until some 50 years ago, had been a strong hold of Christian influence in the Orient, as a result of the work of scores of missionaries. Religion of any kind was banned in the 1940s by the late Kim Il Sung, and replaced with the ideology of socialist self-reliance. Recently when the economy failed and the food crisis became critical, Kim turned to Christians for help because his early education was in a Christian school because his mother had been a Christian convert. The National Council of Churches in America, working with the governments of the U. S. and South Korea pledged help from the United Nations Food Program. When 700 tons of rice was delivered recently, United Methodist Bishop Talbert told the North Koreans, "We are here even though we differ politically because our Christian faith admonishes us to come."[17]

*Speculations About Time*

In preparation for the Global Mission endeavor, Billy Graham discussed the time line of man and projections for the future with every head of state of the free world. In every conversation except one, the leaders expressed the expectation that the world is moving rapidly toward the end of time as we know it. Their judgment is determined by the signs that are predicted in the Scriptures:

- a widespread increase of earthquakes in the world--
    - 14th century - 137
    - 15th century - 174
    - 16th century - 253
    - Since 1971 - 18,000
- great explosion of knowledge, yet confusion about actual truth
- unyielding despair of increasing populations, especially evident in the youth culture, as evidenced in their music, movies, and writing
- cop-out from reality, noted by increase of cults, mystic religions, drug culture, suicide, and euthanasia
- unconquered diseases such as AIDS

- famine and pestilence increases
- wars and rumors of wars as a constant
- unlicensed sexual behavior
- fear and despair among world leaders and scientists.

Many comments paralleling Bertrand Russell's atheistic comment, "I think of suicide, for over man and all his works night falls pitiless and dark."[18]

Jesus said, "As the days of Noah were, so shall the coming of the Son of Man be." We know that God promised that the world would never be destroyed by flooding again, but that the evil elements would be destroyed by fire. We know, too, that we now have weapons that can destroy the entire world by fire.

"These leaders realized in their conversations that the world is caught in a terrible spiritual warfare. It is not a warfare in which we can use manmade weapons; we cannot use guns to settle this kind of war."[19]

For those who believe that God will not punish and will save all mankind "en masse," they ignore the biblical accounts of:

- God, not Noah, closing the door of the ark on those who after extended invitations refused to repent; after having years of God's mercy and patience with their unrighteousness.
- Those who despised Moses's law given by God died without mercy.
- Moses's restriction on entering the Promised Land.
- The destruction of Sodom and Gomorrah.
- The Sixth Seal, described by John in the Revelation, after his vision on the Isle of Patmas.
- God's statements, "Vengeance is mine" and "The Lord will judge His people."
- Refusal of God's mercy and free gift of eternal life means acceptance of God's consequential wrath.

Few realists agree with Bertrand Russell, the famous non-believer, who said, "I do not think Christ was the best and wisest of men, although I grant Him a very high degree of moral goodness. There is one serious defect in Christ's moral character, and that is that He believed in hell. I do not myself feel that any person who is really profoundly humane can believe in everlasting punishment."[20]

## Everyman's Dilemma

If Everyman prides himself on being a realist in his search for truth, there are facts he must face. No matter when time officially ends, according to theologians' predictions or scriptural descriptions, when death, as birth, comes to each of us individually, that is the end of all time for Everyman, be he prince or pauper. Death, though a chilling word, is an integral part of life. Poets hide it in metaphors; composers in dirges and melancholy notes; and artists in shadows and bleak landscapes. But as a part of the sequence of life, it cannot be escaped.

As in the 15th century play, from whose theme I have titled this manuscript, Everyman finds himself alone in his decision as to how he will meet Death, the opposing character in the drama and when that day came, Everyman was abandoned by his former associates whom he had trusted: Fellowship, Kindred, Cousins, Goods, Knowledge, Beauty, Strength, Discretion, and the Five Wits. The only associate who remained with him to the end were Deeds and Charity, interpreted in the Scriptures as Love.

The following projects graphically the dilemma of Everyman as he represents all mankind since Adam. God wants to have a relationship with Everyman.

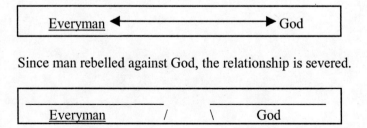

Since man rebelled against God, the relationship is severed.

85

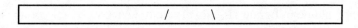

The penalty that <u>Everyman</u> owes is punishable by Death.

To build a bridge for <u>Everyman</u> back to God, Jesus came and paid a debt He did not owe and provided that bridge by His death on the cross.

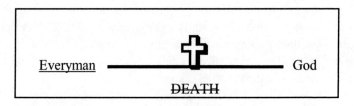

<u>Everyman</u> can choose to establish a relationship with God by utilizing the bridge of the cross to accept His forgiveness and leadership.[21]

But <u>Everyman</u> cannot cross the symbolic bridge until he accepts the fact that the debt he owed was paid by Jesus's blood, in the age old method of cleansing. And he is aware that until he believes and accepts forgiveness that he, like Pilate and Lady McBeth, will not be able to remove the stains of blood from his hands.

# REFERENCES FOR SECTION IV

1. Pierce, John. "Lessons From the Little Nun," The Christian Index Publisher, Atlanta, Georgia, September 5, 1996, p. 6.

2. Bronowski, Jacob. Science and Human Values, Harper and Row Publishers, New York, 1965, p. 45.

3. Frankel, Victor. Man's Search for Meaning, Washington Square Press, New York, 1963, p. 173.

4. Wiesel, Elie. All Rivers Run to the Sea, Knopf Publishing, New York, 1995.

5. Withers, Sarah. "Rejection," The Christian Index, Atlanta, Georgia, March 13, 1997, p. 14.

6. Bostick, Cliff. "The Necessary Function of Religion," Creative Loafing (newspaper), Atlanta, Georgia, March 22, 1997.

7. Munsey, William E. Eternal Retribution, Sword of the Lord Publishing, Murfreesboro, Tennessee, 1951, p. 65.

8. Life and Work Ventures, Southern Baptist Publishing, Nashville, Tennessee, July-September 1995, p. 105.

9. Lawrence, David. "Salvation by Works or Grace," North Peachtree Messenger, October 1991, p. 7.

10. Scott, Carol S. Dunwoody United Methodist Church Bulletin, Dunwoody, Georgia, February 23, 1993.

11. Greene, Michael. Who Is This Jesus, Thomas Nelson Publishers, Nashville, Tennessee, 1992.

12. World Goodwill International Publication, "Preparation for the Reappearance of Christ," London, England, 1951, p. 5.

13. Billy Graham Evangelistic Association Publishing, <u>Decision</u>, Spring 1995 and 1996, Minneapolis, Minnesota, Box 779.

14. Horowitz, Michael of the Hudson Institute as reported on the James Kennedy television program, channel 19, on March 23, 1997.

15. Dart, John. "The Rush to Repent," Atlanta Journal-Constitution, July 1, 1995, p. F6.

16. Associated Press article, "Communist Turns to Jesus to Put Party Back on Top," <u>The Kansas City Star</u> (newspaper), September 24, 1995, p. A-9.

17. Slavin, Barbara. "North Korea Opens Doors to U. S. Christians," <u>USA Today</u>, February 26, 1997, p. 11A.

18. Kennedy, James. <u>Why I Believe the Bible</u>, Word Books Publishing, Waco, Texas, 1981, pp. 153-156.

19. Graham, Billy. "Are You Ready for the Last Day," <u>Decision Magazine</u>, September 1995, pp. 1-3.

20. Russell, Bertrand. <u>Why I Am Not A Christian</u>, Simon and Shuster Publishing, New York, 1967, p. 17.

21. By permission: Mittleberg, Lee and Bill Hybek. <u>Becoming a Contagious Christian</u>, Zondervan Publishing House, Grand Rapids, Michigan, 1995, pp. 65-66.

# SECTION V

# EVERYMAN'S DECISION IS A CHOICE

Life is a series of decisions. Dr. Jim Johnson, Pastor of the Dunwoody Baptist Church, Atlanta, Georgia, describes it this way: "Your life is the sum of your choices." Other than birth, about which no person has his choice, as a citizen in a republic, from the earliest age Everyman has filled his days with minor choices increasing with age to major decisions, which influence not only himself, but the welfare of all who are remotely associated with him.

Everyman may spend 20 or more years preparing for his profession or vocation and yet resist making a decision about his relationship to God, through his decision about Jesus whom God sent for the specific purpose of serving Everyman. The bridge that he must cross to establish that relationship involves his answer to Pilate's question, "What shall I do with Jesus?"

Jesus does not abide neutrality; to not decide is a decision--it is a choice. God gave us a free will to use; not to let atrophy.

*Prodigal Son's Offer Still Open*

Perhaps the most significant story that Jesus told was the story of the Prodigal Son. The father Jesus described said, "You are free to go and you are free to come." It shows that loves does not control or manipulate. This parable teaches a second thing about the nature of God's love--he is not a rescuer. The father does not send a package to the far country where his son has gone, though news of his son's plight probably reached him.

The son knows the way home, and the father gives the son the dignity of managing his own life. The turning point in the parable is when the son in the far country "comes to himself," which, of course, means when he assesses his situation and says, "I am starving. My father's hired servants live better than this. I can't go back as his son again, but since my father is a compassionate man, I will go back and ask to be one of his servants."

When he did arrives, he could not believe the joyous reception he received. Not only was he forgiven for his digressions, but the fatted calf was killed and a ring was placed on his finger in gratitude that the son had made the decision to come home to re-establish his relationship with his father. This story teaches many things, but in Everyman's case, it means that he can make the decision to come just as he is, at any time, and he will be welcomed in the same fashion that the Prodigal Son was received. Everyman is free to say that Micah, Elijah, and Joshua were wrong in their prophesies; that John the Baptist was wrong; that Jesus was wrong; and that the Scriptures and all of the New Testament, which identifies the verification of the early prophet's predictions, are wrong. He can say whatever he wishes; however, that attitude doesn't change anything. A thing is true because it is true or false because it is false. What one chooses to believe or not believe has nothing to do with the veracity of truth.[1]

Everyman must realize that making a good decision is impossible if he closes the door through which truth and wisdom enter. Everyman knows that he must "seek if he is to find" truthful answers for his decision. Whether or not he wants a relationship with Jesus, he will face Him on his last day for that someday will arrive.

When Jesus was on earth, He waited to be discovered and only in the last days before His death did he speak directly to His disciples about who He is. Even today, He waits courteously at the door of Everyman's heart, knocking and patiently waiting to hear the latch turn from the inside allowing admittance. As in the painting by William Hollman Hunt, The Light of the World, which hangs at Keble College, Oxford, He today stands at Everyman's door saying, "If any man hears my voice and opens the door, I will come in to him and have communion with him."

Dr. Criswell reminds us that "In the eternal fact of life and experience, as we learn of Esau, who chose to sell his birthright, we too can sell out our opportunity for the guidance of the Holy Spirit here on earth and the blessed promise of eternal life for the figurative `bowl of porridge' of convenience and procrastination."[2]

*In Addition to Truths, Everyman Reviews Observations*

As Everyman in the ageless Dutch-English drama faces the certainty of Death, he senses an urgency and a measure of insecurity because he realizes that there is "only a small slice of time which gives him a chance to make choices. So much of life is doled out to getting educated and socialized; to career seeking; to work; to building and supporting a family. At that point, reality hits him-- that with the tragedies of plane crashes, heart attacks, drive-by shootings, and untreatable, deadly viruses, that people are dying at all ages, and that someday will be his last day."[3]

As Edward Fitzgerald wrote in his translation of the Rubaiyat of Omar Khayejam, "The moving finger writes: and having writ moves on. Nor all your piety, no wit can lure it back to cancel half a line. Nor all your tears wash out a word of it."[4]

Now, when Everyman readies himself to finalize his decision about his soul's destiny, he reviews and summarizes the observations he has made, in addition to the actual truths he has verified.

- He knows that the friends who said, "It doesn't matter what you believe about Jesus" would be the first to say, "It matters what you believe about civil rights or communism." But God has seen fit to make belief in His Son the prerequisite to His gift of eternal life. So, regardless of the views of his friends, he faces the conviction of the truths he has found and knows now that he must make his own decision regardless of the consequences to his relationships.

- He is aware that the fear of being different, like most fears, tend to diminish as one takes a good look; for at the bottom of most fears lies an intense pre-occupation with self. Also, much of the fear that we shrink from is imaginary. So, if we are to be true to ourselves, it often requires summoning the courage to be different in response to our convictions.[5]

- Jesus's unusualness has inspired insistent belief or total derision because He is totally different from every other seer before or since. If He were just like other historical figures of human history, He could be flicked away, but all time is recorded on the calendar from His birth; inaugurations, deaths, funerals, dedications, and wedding ceremonies express the conscience of His teachings. When He came into the world, there were few, if any, institutions of mercy; no hospitals, refuges for the poor, homes for orphans, or havens for the forsaken. But wherever true Christianity has gone, there are institutions to continue the activities He performed to serve these needs when He was on earth.[6]

- The derision Jesus suffered early on continues to this day, for He did not follow the pattern expected of a political leader, of an intellectual, or of an established religious guru. The educated were shocked at Jesus's depth of learning, though He had never studied at their formal schools. They knew that God had spoken to Moses, but they questioned whereby that Jesus got His authority to speak. Most of all, when the multitudes followed Him, they feared that He, as a Jewish representative leader, would attempt to take over the government and give them serious trouble with Rome.[7]

- But as C. S. Lewis states, "If we accept that Jesus died, He must have been human like each of us. If one accepts the evidence (as C. S. Lewis and Simon Greenleaf) that He was resurrected to immortal life, one cannot deny that He was God's Son. And if one accepts that He was who He said He was, then His promises, His warnings, and His instructions must be heeded."[8]

- Everyman is aware that "Strikingly, nearly 80 percent of Americans of various religious faiths, and some of none, say that they believe in life after death and two-thirds feel certain that there is a heaven. Despite the apparent contradiction, during the past half century science has moved from a dogmatic denial of realities beyond its reach toward an appreciation of their possibility.

Dialogue between scientists and theologians has become increasingly common. From Albert Einstein to Stephen Hawkins, scientists have grown more comfortable in using the word God in pondering questions of meaning and order."[9]

- Charles Colson says in his book, <u>Loving God</u>, "When you come to the decision that you believe in Jesus, it becomes simple: you repent of your former unbelief and in appreciation you obey and you serve according to His direction."

- <u>Everyman</u> balances God's unyielding demand for retribution with the knowledge that His love is expressed in giving man an alternative to death. "His boundless love found a way to satisfy the demand of justice and to provide an escape for the condemnation of sin, at the great cost of letting His Son bear the punishment <u>Everyman</u> deserves."[10]

- When it comes to doubts, <u>Everyman</u> realizes that one must hand his doubts over to God, just as he has learned to hand over his other temptations--such as temper, pride, bad habits, and worry. God always takes possession of a surrendered will and gives it peace.

"As a researcher for truth repeatedly substantiates his findings in the records, research findings, experiences, thoughts, and writings of some of the most learned and inspired persons of the ages, there finally came a time for each of them--a day--that each alone had to respond to the same question that <u>Everyman</u> since Pilate has had to answer. <u>Everyman</u> knows that his helplessness to change the past is exceeded only by his total helplessness to change the future beyond that `last day' that will come to all, as described in Ecclesiastes 11:3, 'As the tree falls, so shall it lie.'"[11]

*Time Runs Out*

Everyman remembers the slang question, "Can 50,000 Frenchmen be wrong?" And he says, "Can all these knowledgeable, and often inspired, believers be wrong? Could all of those hundreds of specific descriptions of the Messiah made by the inspired prophets so revered in the Old Testament--and were all fulfilled at that probability of one in 100,000,000,000,000,000,000 in one life be strangely incorrect? It's beyond all reason.

Everyman knows that since time has placed him on this side of Jesus's cross that his responsibility for an answer is far greater than for Pilate: for centuries of conclusive proof of who Jesus is gives knowledge for a decision that Pilate did not have.

Yes, 20 wide centuries have come and gone. Times have changed; circumstances have altered, but He abideth. Jesus is the same yesterday, today, and tomorrow. "His was the ark which saved Noah. He provided the blood of the Passover and the Amazing Grace described by the former slave trader. He is the centerpiece of the human race and the inspiration at the head of the column of the progress of mankind."[12]

And so Everyman now knows that he nor NO man can ever escape answering Pilate's question:

### WHAT SHALL I DO WITH JESUS?

# References for Section V

1. Editor, <u>North Peachtree Messenger</u>, November 1989, p. 71.

2. Criswell, W. A. <u>Five Great Questions of the Bible</u>, Zondervan Publishing Company, Grand Rapids, Michigan, 1958, p. 50.

3. Poole, Charles E. <u>Don't Cry Past Tuesday</u>, Smith and Helweys Publishing, Greenville, South Carolina, 1994, p. 86.

4. Criswell, ibid, p. 50.

5. Graham, Billy. "Gentle, Good and Faithful," <u>Decision</u>, March 1995, p. 1.

6. Krohl, Paul. <u>Who Was Jesus</u>? Worldwide Church of God, Thomas Nelson Publishing, Pasadena, California, 1982, p. 3.

7. Lewis, C. S. <u>The Case for Christianity</u>, Macmillan Publishing Company, New York, 1989, p. 50.

8. Shuler, Jeffrey. "Heaven in the Age of Reason," <u>U. S. News and World Report</u>, March 31, 1997, p. 66.

9. Romman, Edward. "The Choice is Ours," <u>Decision</u>, October 1995, p. 34.

10. Criswell, ibid.

11. Ibid.

12. Ibid.

# APPENDIX

## A LOOK AT SOME OF THE 456 OLD TESTAMENT PROPHESIES

Recent studies by biblical scholars indicate that there are 456 prophesies concerning the Messiah. What are the laws of probability on the fulfillment of these prophesies? Peter Stoner wrote an article on this in <u>Science Speaks</u> (Moody Press, 1963) in which he considered eight of the prophesies:

1. The place of the Messiah's birth;
2. His being preceded by a messenger;
3. How He was to enter Jerusalem;
4. His betrayal by an associate;
5. He would be betrayed for 30 pieces of silver;
6. The money would be thrown in God's house;
7. He would be mute before His accusers;
8. He would be crucified.

Stoner reported that by using the modern science of probability in reference to these eight prophesies, "we find that the chance that one man might have lived down to the present time and fulfilled all eight of these prophesies is one in ten to the 17th power. To help us better comprehend this statistic, that would be 1 in 100,000,000,000,000,000."

The above is used by special permission of Chosen Books, a division of Baker Book House Co., Grand Rapids, Michigan from page 125 of Stan Telchin's Book, <u>Betrayed</u>, published in 1984 by <u>Chosen Books</u>.

The following is a sample of the type of prophesies and fulfillments concerning Jesus used by such theological researchers as Mr. Stoner.

The scriptural quotes in the following are taken from the Revised Standard Version of Tyndale-King James Bible. This version, copyrighted in the mid 20$^{th}$ century, is based on 20$^{th}$ century knowledge of the Hebrew and Greek texts, as well as currently accepted English word meanings.

This sample of prophesies was prepared by the author, with the assistance of Rev. Robert Banks and Harold Banister

# The Lineage of Jesus

## Old Testament Prophesies

According to <u>Moses</u>:
   Genesis 22:15, 18
"and the angel of the Lord called to Abraham - - - 'By your descendents shall all nations of the earth bless themselves, because you have obeyed my voice.'"

According to <u>Jeremiah</u>:
   Jeremiah 23:5
"Behold the days are coming says the Lord, when I will raise up for David a righteous branch, and he shall reign as king, and deal wisely, and shall execute justice and righteousness in all the land."

According to <u>David</u>:
   Psalms 2:6,
"I have set my king on Zion, my holy hill."
"Jesus...the son of Isaac..."
(Luke 3:23,24)

## New Testament Fulfillment

According to <u>Matthew</u>:
   Matthew 1:17
"So all the generation from Abraham to David were 14 generations, and from David to the deportation to Babylon 14 generations, and from the deportation to Babylon to Christ is 14 generations.

According to <u>Luke</u>:
   Luke 3:23, 31-34 and 38
"Jesus when He began his ministry was about 30 years of age, being the son of David, Jesse, Judah, Jacob, Isaac, Abraham, Enos, Seth, Adam, the Son of God."

According to <u>Mark</u>:
   Mark 15:25-26
"When they crucified Him the inscription of the charge against Him read 'The King of the Jews'."

## Psalm 2:7

"I will tell of the decree of the Lord: He said to me, 'You are my Son, today I have begotten you. Ask me and I will make nations your heritage'."

## Mark 1:9-11

"Jesus came from Nazareth of Galilee and was baptized in the River Jordan by John. And when He came up out of the water He saw the heavens open up and the Spirit descending on Him like a dove, and a voice came from heaven, 'Thou are my beloved Son in whom I am well pleased'."

## The Miracles of Jesus

According to Isaiah:

Isaiah 35:5

"The eyes of the blind shall be opened and the ears of the deaf unstopped; oh then shall the lame leap like a hart, and the tongue of the dumb sing for joy."

According to Matthew:

Matthew 9:35

"And Jesus went about all the cities and villages teaching in their synagogues, and preaching the gospel of the kingdom and healing every disease and infirmity."

## Teaching by Parables

According to David:

Psalms 98: 1-2

"Give ear, oh my people to my teaching. I will open my mouth in a parable."

According to Matthew:

Matthew 13:34

"All this Jesus said to the crowds in parables; indeed, He said nothing to them without a parable. This was to fulfill what was written by the prophet: 'I will open my mouth in a parable. I will utter what has been hidden since the foundation of the world'."

# Jesus Betrayal by Judas

According to <u>David</u>:
Psalms 41:7
"Even my bosom friend in whom I trusted, who ate of my bread has lifted his heel against me."

According to <u>Luke</u>:
Luke 22:21
"For behold the hand of him who betrays me is with me at the table."

According to <u>Mark</u>:
Mark 14:43-45
"Now the betrayer had given them a sign saying, 'The one I kiss is the man; seize him.' He went up to him at once and said 'Master'. And he kissed Him."

According to <u>Zachariah</u>:
Zachariah 11:12-13
"And they weighed out as my wages 30 shekels of silver."
"Then the Lord said to me, 'Cast it into the treasury.' So I took the 30 shekels of silver and cast them into the treasury in the house of the Lord."

According to <u>Matthew</u>:
Matthew 25:14-15
"Judas Iscariot went to the Chief Priests and said, 'What will you give me to deliver him to you?' And they paid him 30 pieces of silver."

Matthew 27: 3,5
--- "he repented and brought back the 30 pieces of silver to the Chief Priests saying, 'I have sinned in betraying innocent blood.' And throwing down the pieces of silver in the temple, he departed and went out and hanged himself."

## Jesus' Trial and Tribulation

According to <u>Zachariah</u>:
   Zachariah 13:7
"Strike my shepherd and my sheep may be scattered."

According to <u>Isaiah</u>:
   Isaiah 53:6
"All we like sheep have gone astray.  We have turned everyone to his own way."

   Isaiah 53:7
" ---yet He opened not His mouth, like a lamb that is led to the slaughter, and like a sheep that before it's shearer is dumb, so He opened not His mouth."

   Isaiah 50:5-6
"I was not rebellious.  I turned not backward.  I gave my back to the smitters.  I hid not my face from shame and spitting."

According to <u>Mark</u>:
   Mark 14:50
"They all forsook Him and fled."

   Mark 14:4-5
"And Pilate again asked Him, 'Have you no answer to make?  See how many charges they bring against you.'  But Jesus made not answer.

   Mark 15:19-20
"They struck His head with a reed, and spat upon Him.  And when they had mocked Him they stripped Him of the purple robe, put His clothes on Him and led Him out to crucify Him."

According to <u>Isaiah</u>:
Isaiah 53:12
"Yet He bore the sins of many, and made intercession for the transgressors."

According to <u>David</u>:
Psalm 22:16-18
"A company of evildoers encircle me, and they pierced my hands and feet. --- they divided my garments among them and for my raiment they cast lots."

Psalm 69:4
"More in number than the hairs of my head are they that hate me without cause."

Psalm 69:21
"They gave me poison for food, and for my thirst they gave me vinegar to drink."

Psalm 22:1
"My God! My God! Why hast Thou forsaken me?"

According to <u>Luke</u>:
Luke 23:34
"And Jesus said, 'Father forgive them for they know not what they do'."

According to <u>Mark</u>:
Mark 15:22,24
"And they brought Him to the place called Golgotha --- And they crucified Him, and divided His garments among them casting lots for them."

According to <u>John</u>:
John 15:24
"And now they have seen and hated both me and my Father. It is to fulfill the word that is written in their law. They hated me without cause."

John 19:25
"Jesus said 'I thirst.' They put a sponge full of the vinegar on a hyssop and held it to His mouth."

According to <u>Matthew</u>:
Matthew 27:25
"Jesus cries, 'Eli, Eli lama, sabach-thani' that is my God, why hast Thou forsaken me?"

Psalm 34:20
"He keeps all His bones, not one of them is broken."

According to <u>John</u>:
John 19:33
"And when they came to Jesus and saw that He was already dead, they did not break his legs."

# Jesus' Death

According to <u>David</u>:
    Psalm 31:5
"Into thy hands I commit my spirit; Thou hast redeemed me."

According to <u>Luke</u>:
    Luke 23:46
"Then Jesus crying with a loud voice said, 'Father into thy hands I commit my spirit.' And having said that He breathed His last.

According to <u>Zachariah</u>:
    Zachariah 12:10
"I will pour out on the House of David a spirit of compassion and supplication so that when they look on whom they pierced they will mourn for Him."

According to <u>John</u>:
    John 19:34
"But one of the soldiers pierced His side with a spear and at once came out blood and water."

According to <u>David</u>:
    Psalm 38:11
"My friends and companions stand aloof from my plague and my kinsman stand afar off."

According to <u>Mark</u>:
    Mark 15:20
"And there were also women looking on from afar, among them Mary Magdalene, and Mary the Mother of Jesus and Salome."

According to <u>Amos</u>:
    Amos 8:9
"And on that day says the Lord God, 'I will make the sun to go down at noon, and darken the earth in broad daylight."

According to <u>Luke</u>:
    Luke 23:44-45
"About the sixth hour there was darkness over the whole land until the ninth hour. While the sun's light failed and the curtain of the temple was torn in two."

According to Isaiah:

Isaiah 53:9

"And they made His grave with the wicked, and with a rich man in His death."

According to Matthew:

Matthew 27:57

"When it was evening there came a rich man from Arimathea, named Joseph, who was also a disciple of Jesus and he went to Pilate and asked for the body. Pilate ordered it to be given to him."

# About the Author

Received undergraduate degree Asheville College & Univ, of Tenn. Masters & Doctorate Univ. of Georgia. Post doctoral study: Univ. of Calif., Univ. of Keele in the U.K. & as a National Science Fellow at the Univ. of Colorado. Served as a classroom teacher in 3 states & for Atomic Energy Comm.

Director of Teacher Corp & Dir. of Program Development, Atlanta Public Sch.; Prof. of Education, Univ. of Georgia: Assoc. State Superintendent of Georgia Schools. Directed 3 programs which were written into the - U.S, Congressional Record as exemplary.

Author of 3 books and joint author of 3 texts in education. As a charter member of World Council for Curriculum & Instruction and as U.S. National Pres. of the 150,000 Member Assoc. of Supervision & Curriculum Dev. worked with the Ministers of Educ. in Canada, New Zealand, Australia. China, Japan, U.K., Russia and Pacific Basin UNESCO.

Listed in Who's Who of American Women; World Who's Who of Women; International Biography of 2000 Women of Achievement; Foremost Women of the 20th Century & International Directory of Distinguished Leaders.